SAVING FOXES

PORTRAITS *of* RESCUED FOXES *and* THEIR STORIES

by LAUREN WILLIAMSON

photography by MIKAYLA RAINES, KIM DAVIS, BRUCE COOLEN, *and* ALEXIS HOWARD

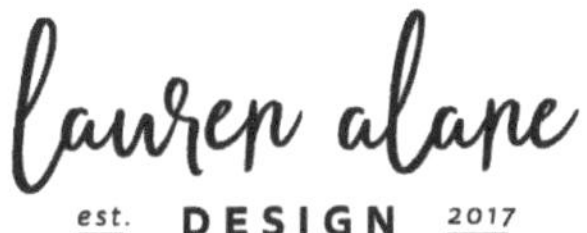

ISBN: 978-1-7342728-1-9

Written and designed by Lauren Williamson

Edited by Joelle Williamson

Cover photo © 2019 Kim Davis

Cover design by Lauren Williamson

Photos on pages 7, 8, 9, 10, 12, 13, 14, 15, 19, 22, 23, 28-29, 32, 33, 34, 38, 40, 41, 42, 43, 52, 53, 54-55, 57, 58, 59, 60, 62, 63, 66-67, 69, 71, 73, 74, 78, 79, 82, 84-85, 88-89, 92, 96-97, 99, 100 © 2019 Mikayla Raines

Photos on pages 3, 4, 6, 16-17, 30, 31, 44, 45, 46, 47, 48, 50, 51, 64, 80, 81, 87 © 2019 Kim Davis

Photos on pages 20-21, 24-25, 26-27, 36, 37, 56, 70, 72, 76-77, 93, 94, 98-99, 101 © 2019 Bruce Coolen

Photos on pages 90-91, 95 © 2019 Alexis Howard

Lauren Alane Design LLC
lauren.alane.design@gmail.com
laurenalanedesign.com

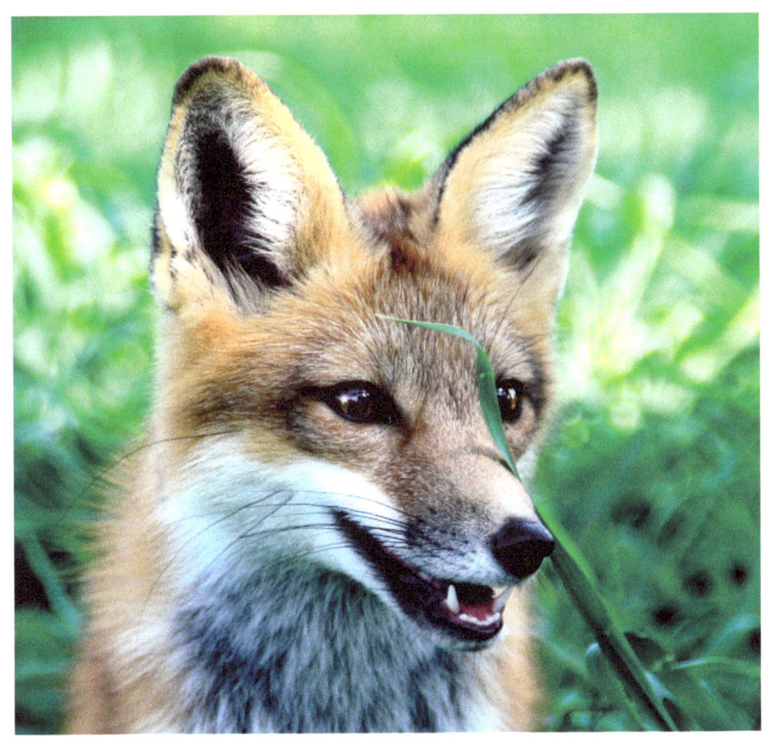

INTRODUCTION

The following collection of photographs and stories capture the unique and vibrant personalities of 27 foxes who came through the doors of Save a Fox rescue between 2016-2019. This book was made possible by the donated time, skills, and captivating photographs from passionate volunteers and fox enthusiasts around the world. All net proceeds from this book go directly to Save a Fox, supporting their mission to continue rescuing these beautiful creatures.

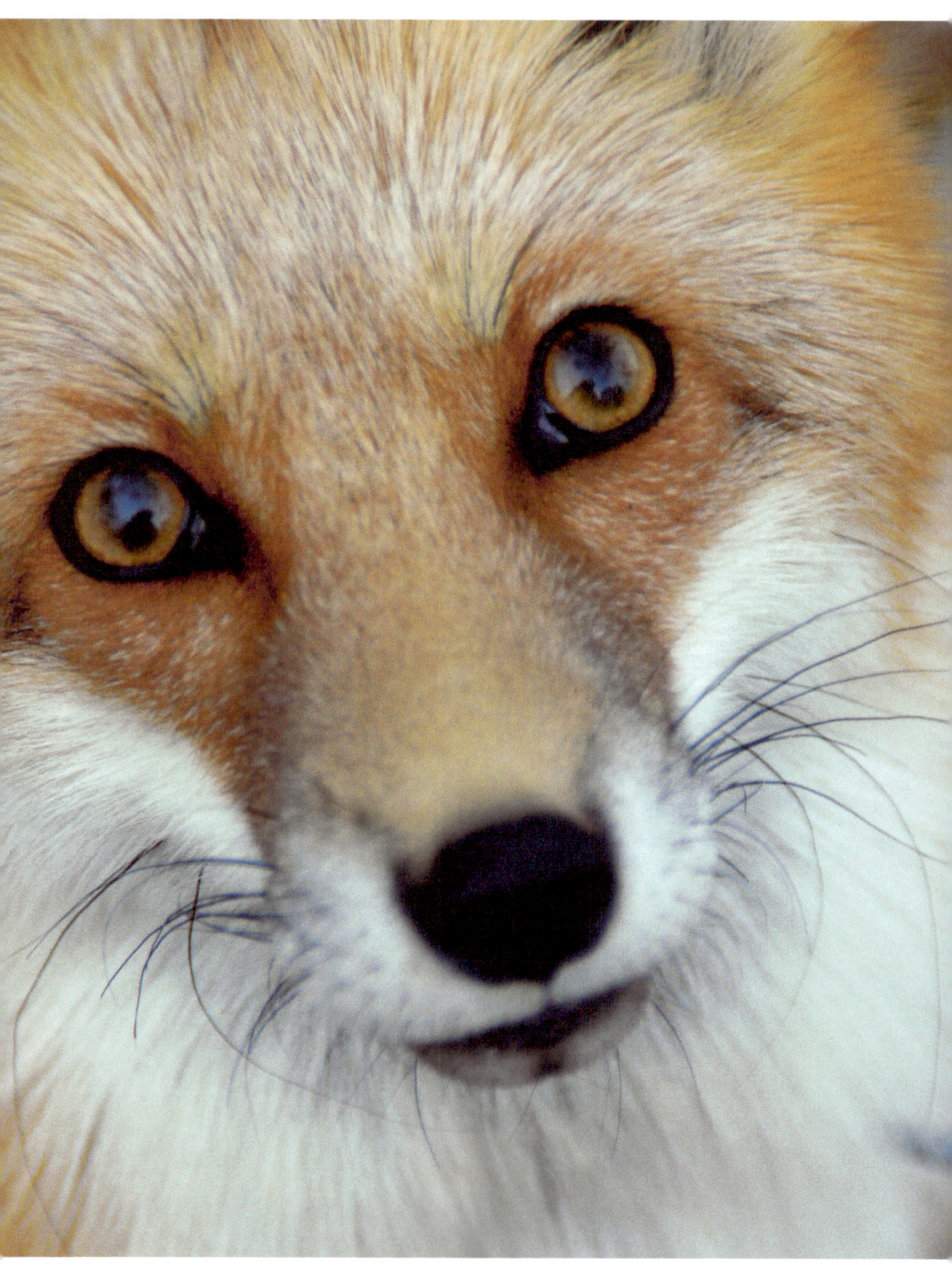

CONTENTS

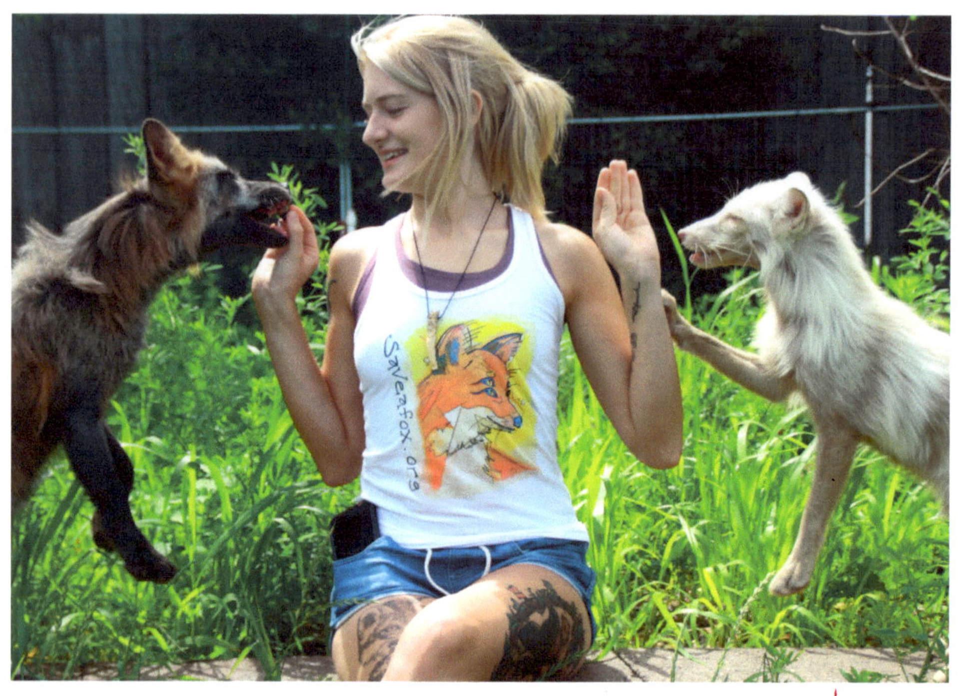

ABOUT SAVE A FOX

Save a Fox is the largest fox rescue in the U.S. The non-profit, donation-funded organization sits on several acres of land in rural Minnesota, allowing foxes room to run freely and feel as "wild" as possible. Most of the rescue's animals are saved from fur farms, where they would have been killed for their fur, used for breeding, or euthanized due to illness or damaged pelts. Save a Fox also takes in pet foxes who were surrendered to the rescue by owners who got in over their heads with the challenges of fox care—a situation that is, unfortunately, all too common.

Since all of the foxes that come through Save a Fox's doors have been captive-bred for generations, they lack the instincts necessary to survive on their own, and can never be released into the wild. Once the foxes are ready, the rescue's goal is to adopt them out into safe, loving, fox-knowledgeable homes. This way, Save a Fox has room to continue rescuing more animals.

Although foxes are the rescue's focus, occasionally Save a Fox takes in other animals in need, including minks, raccoons, squirrels, snakes, sugar gliders, opossum, cats, a coyote, and even a bobcat.

SAVE A FOX'S BEGINNINGS

Save a Fox owner Mikayla Raines' passion for foxes began at the age

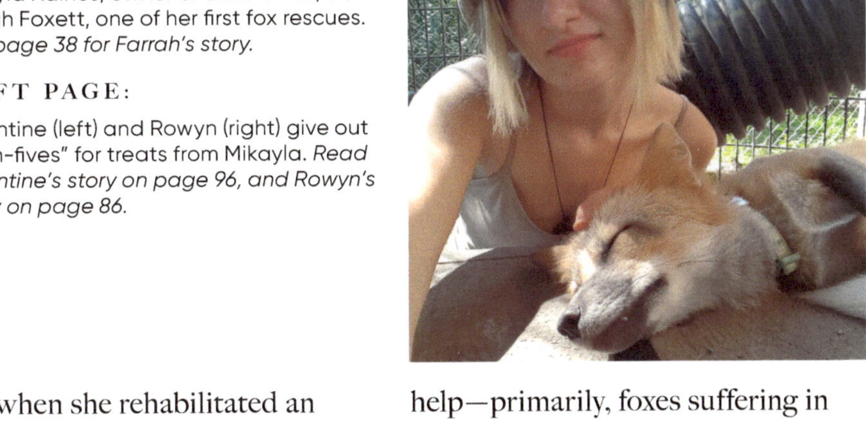

of 15, when she rehabilitated an orphaned gray fox kit she found crying and alone in her backyard. She named him Nikko. And, although she didn't know it at the time, this little fox was the first of many that would come into her life.

A few years later, Mikayla had passed her wildlife rehabilitation courses and was working as a wildlife rehabber when a domestic fox breeder gave her a red fox kit that was suffering from a life-threatening infection. Mikayla named the kit Farrah Foxett, and bottle-raised her back to health at her home. Since Farrah was bred to be a pet, she couldn't be released into the wild, and lived the rest of her life with Mikayla.

After rescuing Farrah, Mikayla became aware of other situations where domestic foxes needed help—primarily, foxes suffering in fur farms. Mikayla got in touch with local fur farmers, asking if she could take in their unwanted foxes. Her first fur farm rescues were 3 tiny kits who were rejected by their mother, and therefore not wanted by the fur farmer anymore. Today, Mikayla continues working with local fur farmers who choose to surrender their unwanted foxes to her rather than euthanizing them.

In 2017, Save a Fox became a registered 501(c)(3) charity. The rescue has grown substantially since its beginnings with Nikko, attracting a vast social media following of hundreds of thousands of fans and followers. None of the rescue's work would be possible without the passionate support of volunteers, sponsors, and fox lovers around the world.

TO LEARN MORE, VISIT SAVEAFOX.ORG OR CONNECT ON SOCIAL MEDIA:

 saveafox_rescue   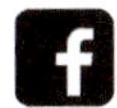 SaveAFoxRescue   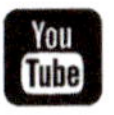 SaveAFox

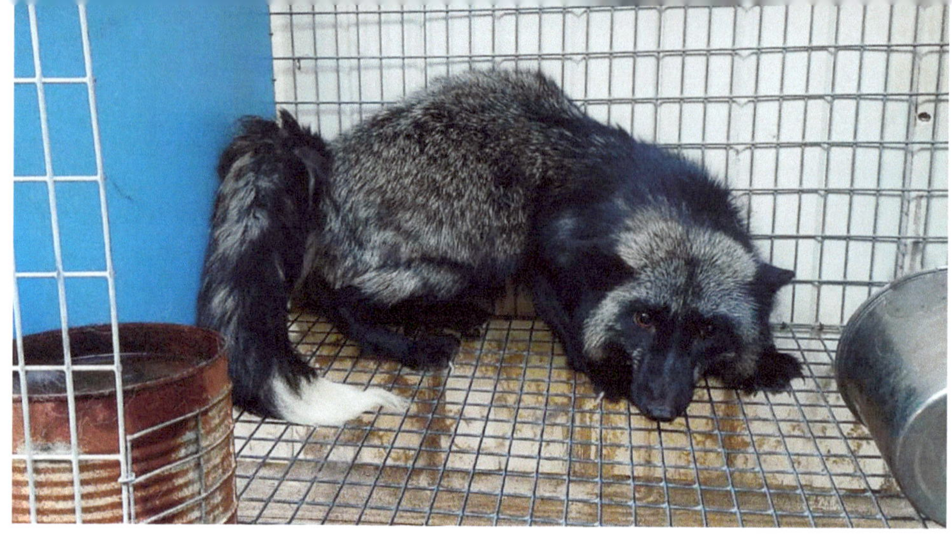

A silver fox cowers in her cage at a fur farm, where many of Save a Fox's rescues come from. This fox, named Scarlett, was rescued by Save a Fox and adopted by an educational center in Minnesota.

ABOUT FUR FARMS

One of the primary reasons Save a Fox was founded was to rescue foxes from fur farms and allow them to live happier and more natural lives. Each year, thousands of animals are raised as livestock on farms and killed for their pelts. These pelts are sold to clothing manufacturers or taxidermists. In the U.S., foxes are one of the most commonly farmed animals in the fur industry, along with mink, ferrets, and raccoons. Fur farm animals grow up in small indoor cages where they can usually only take a few steps in any direction. They often live their entire lives without access to the outdoors or sunlight, as these are seen as elements that could damage their pelts. Many of the animals on fur farms develop abnormal and self-destructive behaviors due to extreme psychological stress.

Unfortunately, fur farms are entirely legal in the U.S. along with dozens of countries around the world, so the vast majority of fur farm animals cannot be saved. However, Mikayla Raines, the owner of Save a Fox, keeps up a business relationship with local fur farmers who choose to surrender their unwanted foxes to her rather than euthanize them. These foxes may be discarded from farms due to birth defects, injuries, or other health problems that would require expensive veterinary care or damage the foxes' pelts.

TO LEARN MORE,
VISIT SAVEAFOX.ORG/
FOXES-AT-FUR-FARMS

ADOPTING FOXES

Save a Fox's primary goal is to place their animals in forever homes so that each fox can receive the individual care it needs, and so that Save a Fox has room to continue rescuing animals. However, even so-called "domestic" pet foxes present much more complex challenges than those of regular companion animals. Not everyone is equipped for fox ownership. Sadly, many of the foxes that come through the rescue's doors are pets who were surrendered by owners who could not give their foxes the extensive level of care they require. For these reasons, careful planning and consideration is crucial before making the decision to adopt a fox.

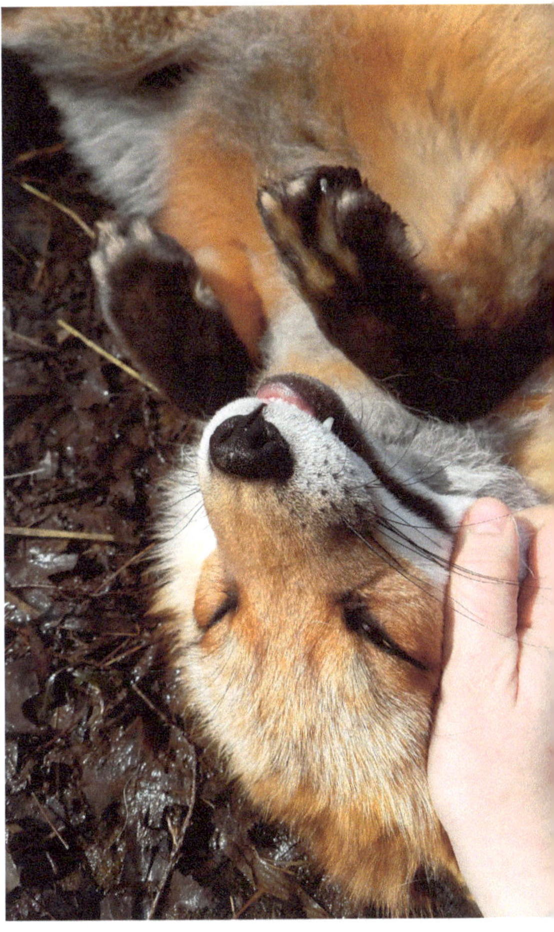

Dixie is one of the most social foxes at the rescue. *Read more about Dixie on page 30.*

TRAINING & BEHAVIOR

Even though captive-bred foxes are too tame to survive in the wild, they are still not fully domesticated like a dog or cat, and need to be respected for their fiercely independent spirits. Foxes usually only bond with a few people, and will be skittish towards strangers. Bonding with a fox requires patience and persistent one-on-one time in order to build trust. With very fearful foxes, this might mean simply sitting quietly in the fox's enclosure without interacting with it until it's used to your presence. This step could take several days, weeks, or even months depending on the fox. Once trust is earned, foxes can learn basic commands with gentle training and lots of treats—but they will only participate in these games when they feel like it. Foxes are also relentless diggers and chewers, and these natural, destructive traits can't be trained out of them. Since foxes are wired to mark their territory, a pet fox will most likely never be fully potty trained, although some fox owners have had success with litterbox training. Foxes only respond to positive reinforcement. They will become fearful and mistrusting if they are yelled at or punished. They need daily exercise and games so that they don't become bored.

For a more thorough article on fox training and behavior, visit saveafox.org/basic-fox-care.

LIVING ARRANGEMENTS

Foxes are very clever escape artists who need a secure space that is at least 60 square feet large. Their outdoor enclosure should have a roof or a guard around the top leaning in at an angle so that the fox can't climb over it. The floor of the enclosure should either be made of concrete, wire mesh, or have a three-foot-deep mesh guard installed around the base of the fence so that the fox can't dig under it.

When a fox is indoors, it must be closely supervised. Foxes can easily climb up onto tables and counters, so everything that is dangerous or fragile in a room needs to be secured behind closed doors.

At Save a Fox, the foxes are kept in secure outdoor pens that include a cozy "den" for sleeping, access to food and water, and a variety of toys and structures to climb on. Throughout the day, the foxes are rotated out into one of several large, securely-fenced yards with one or two other foxes who get along with each other.

For more information on fox enclosures, visit saveafox.org/basic-fox-care.

DIET

Pet foxes require a special grain-free, protein-rich diet that is as similar as possible to what they would eat in the wild. Most brands of dog or cat food do not contain all of the nutrients a fox needs. As omnivores, a fox's diet should

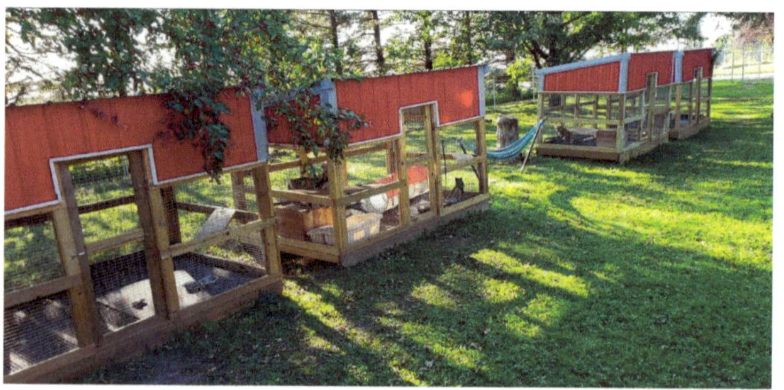

The foxes at Save a Fox stay in secure pens when they are not out in one of several large "fox yards" on the property. Throughout the day, they are socialized with other foxes and played with by volunteers.

include raw meat, fish, or eggs at least every other day, along with a variety of fruits and vegetables.

HEALTH

Another crucial challenge for fox owners is finding a veterinarian who is knowledgeable about foxes. Most regular vets will not see exotic pets. Save a Fox requires that potential adopters list a vet who is capable of seeing the fox on their adoption application. If potential owners do not have a vet lined up, their application will not be accepted.

EXOTIC PET LAWS

Foxes are not allowed to be owned as pets in many areas. Laws regarding fox ownership vary by city, county, and state in the U.S. Not knowing the rules and regulations regarding fox ownership before adopting can have heartbreaking consequences for both owners and their foxes. Many of the foxes at Save a Fox were surrendered to the rescue because their owners ignored or did not research the exotic pet laws in their areas.

SPONSORING FOXES

Sponsoring is another great way to save a fox, especially for people who want to help but don't have the time or space to adopt. Sponsors pay monthly basic care fees and an annual veterinary care fee to support a fox at the rescue. They are allowed to visit their foxes when they want to, and can send extra toys and treats if they wish. Weekly updates on sponsored foxes, including videos and photos, are posted on Instagram and Facebook. Some people decide to co-sponsor foxes, splitting the cost of sponsoring between 2 or more people.

Although sponsored foxes belong to their sponsors, they are still available for adoption. If they weren't, Save a Fox would be at full capacity very quickly and wouldn't be able to save more animals. However, sponsors are allowed to review any promising adoption applications for their foxes before they are accepted. Anyone can sponsor a fox for as long as they want, or until the fox finds a forever home.

TO LEARN MORE ABOUT ADOPTING OR SPONSORING A FOX, VISIT SAVEAFOX.ORG

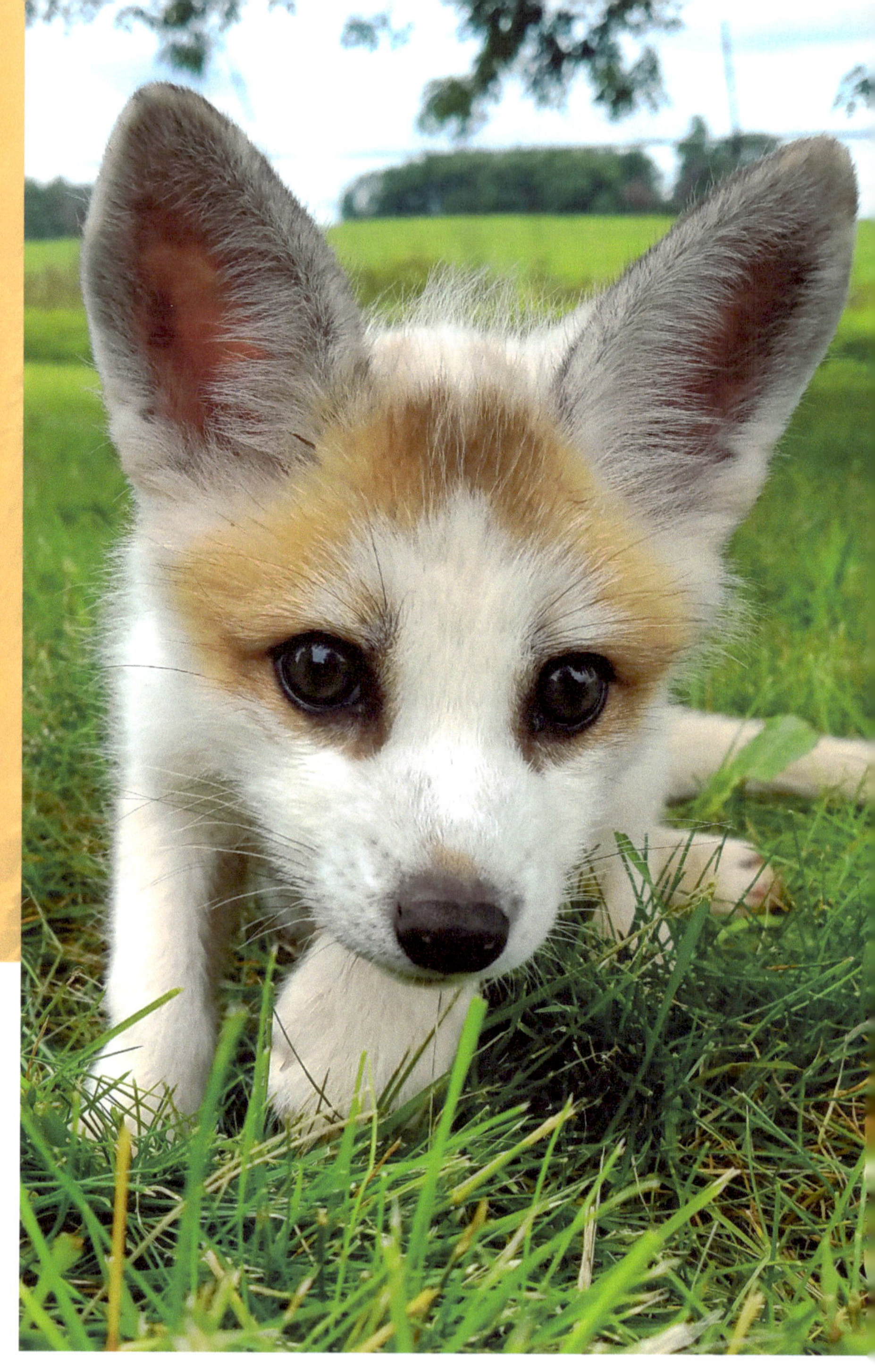

THE MARBLE FOX is actually a color variation of the red fox, not its own species. Like many fox colorations in the pet and fur industries, the marble fox was developed through selective breeding in captivity, and doesn't occur naturally in the wild. Marble foxes are very common in the pet trade.

Artemis

THE MARBLE FOX

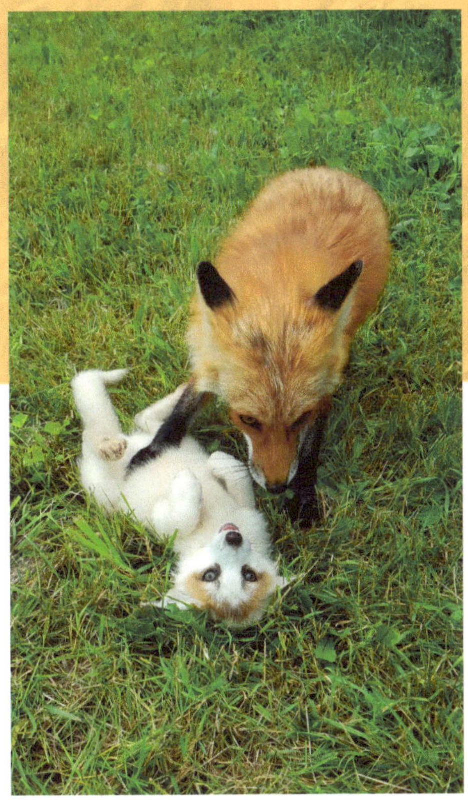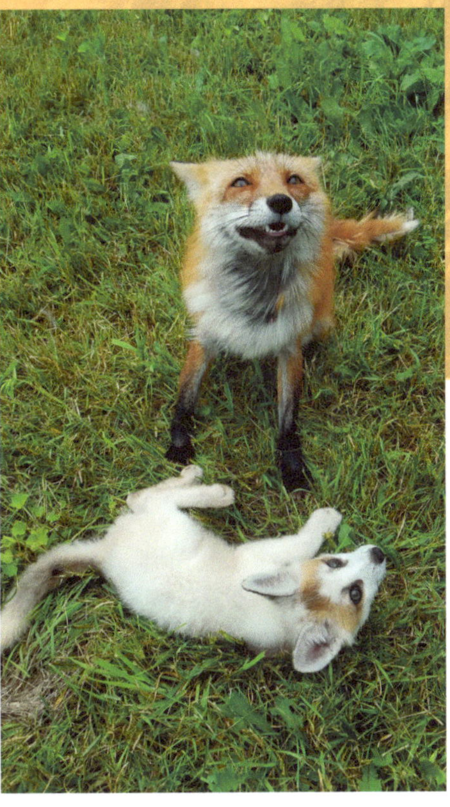

A R T E M I S was rescued from a fur farm after being rejected by his mother. He was adopted as a kit in July of 2018 and renamed Finnick. Another rescued kit, Ash (renamed Auggie) was adopted along with him. Dixie acted as a mother to the kits while they were at the rescue (above). *See Ash's story on page 14, and Dixie's story on page 30.*

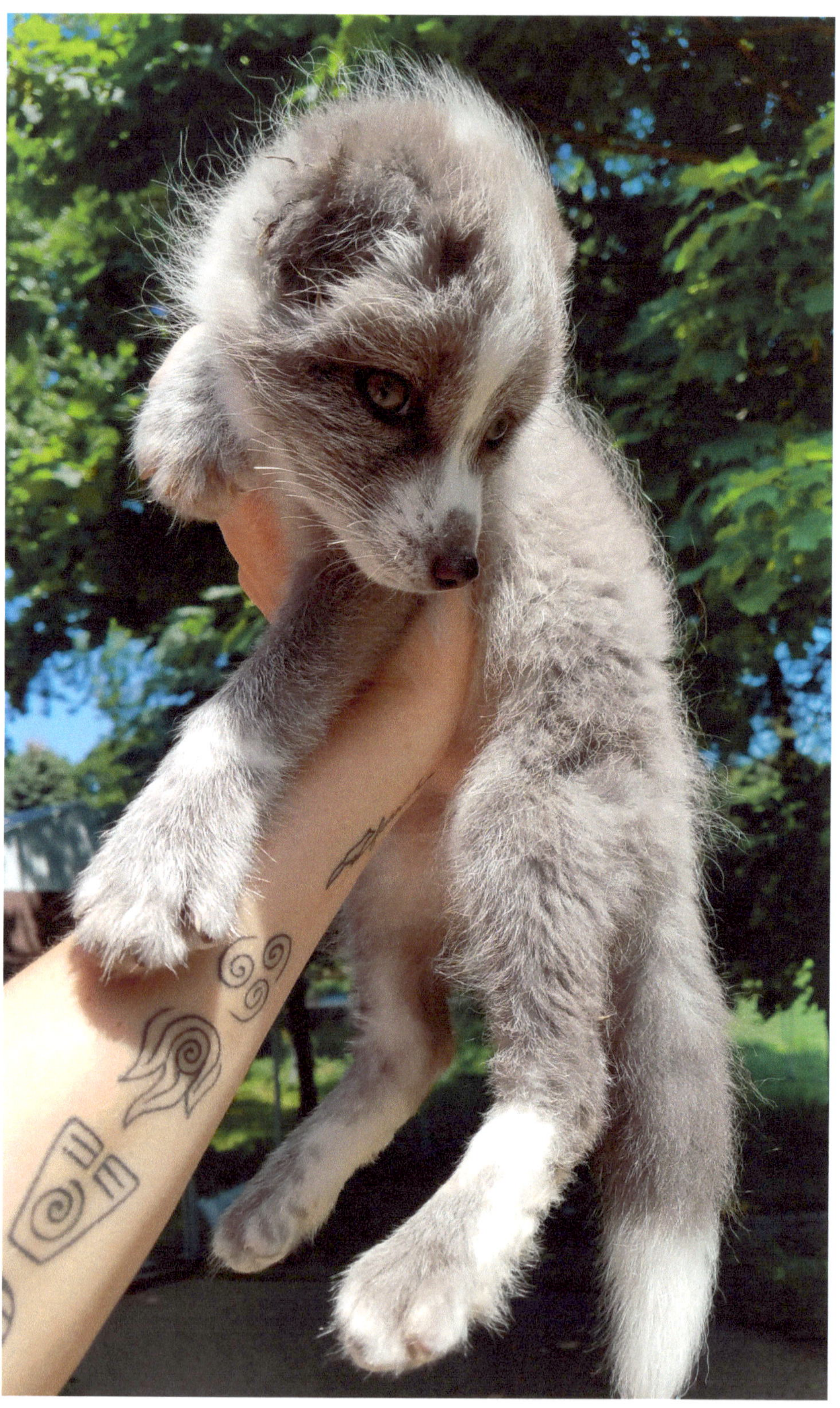

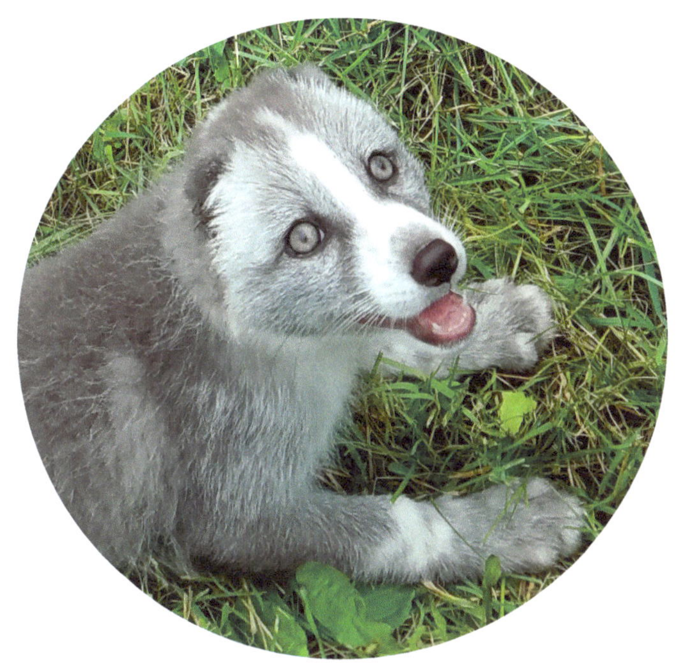

ASH

THE PLATINUM FOX

ASH was born in a fur farm and rescued in the spring of 2018. Oftentimes in fur farms, stressed and traumatized mother foxes "over-groom" their kits, chewing them too harshly and causing harm or even death. This was the case with Ash, who lost both of his ears and was the only surviving kit in his litter. Ash still has some hearing, but he is prone to ear infections. He was renamed Auggie, and was happily adopted along with Artemis (renamed Finnick). *Read Artemis's story on page 12.*

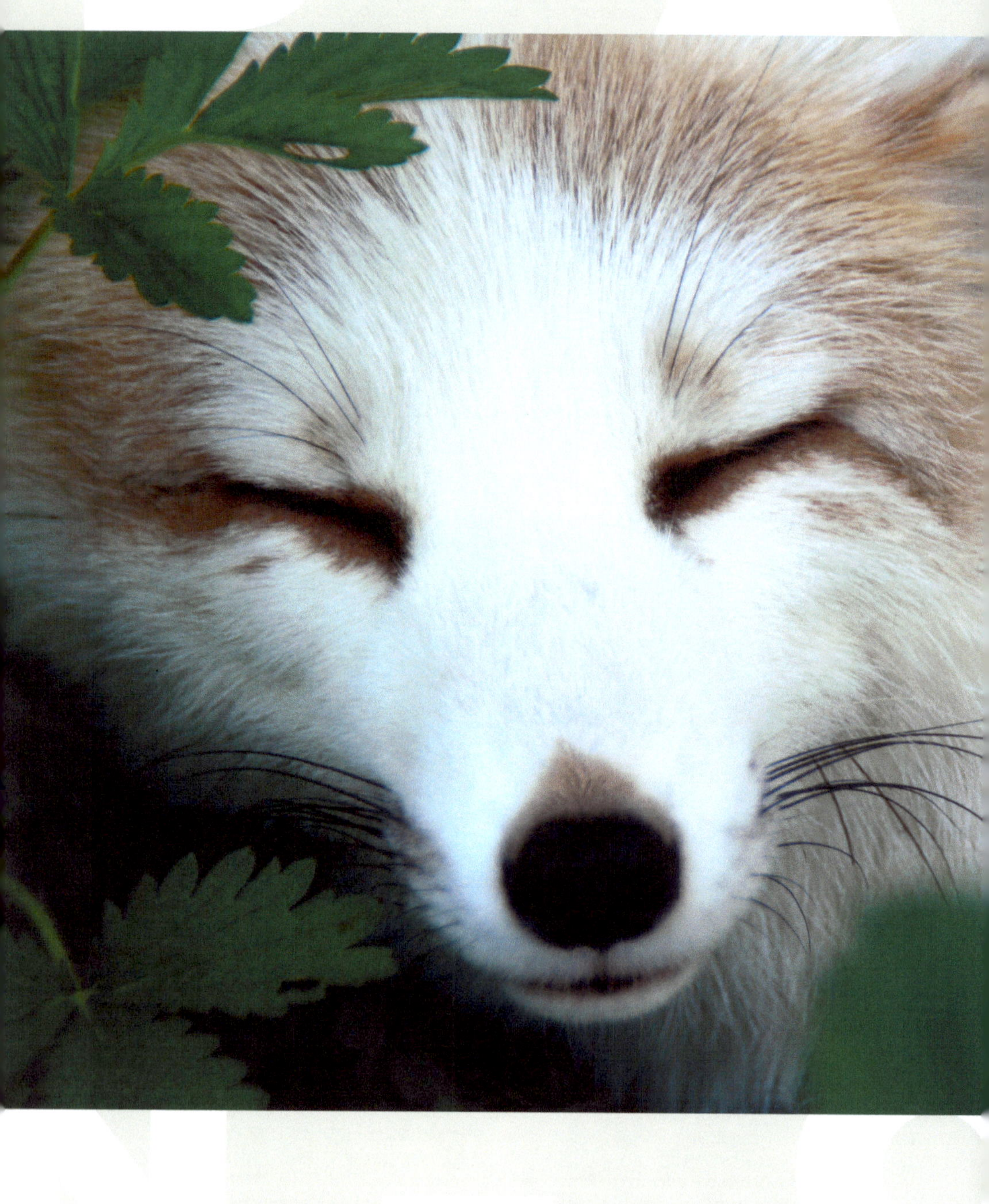

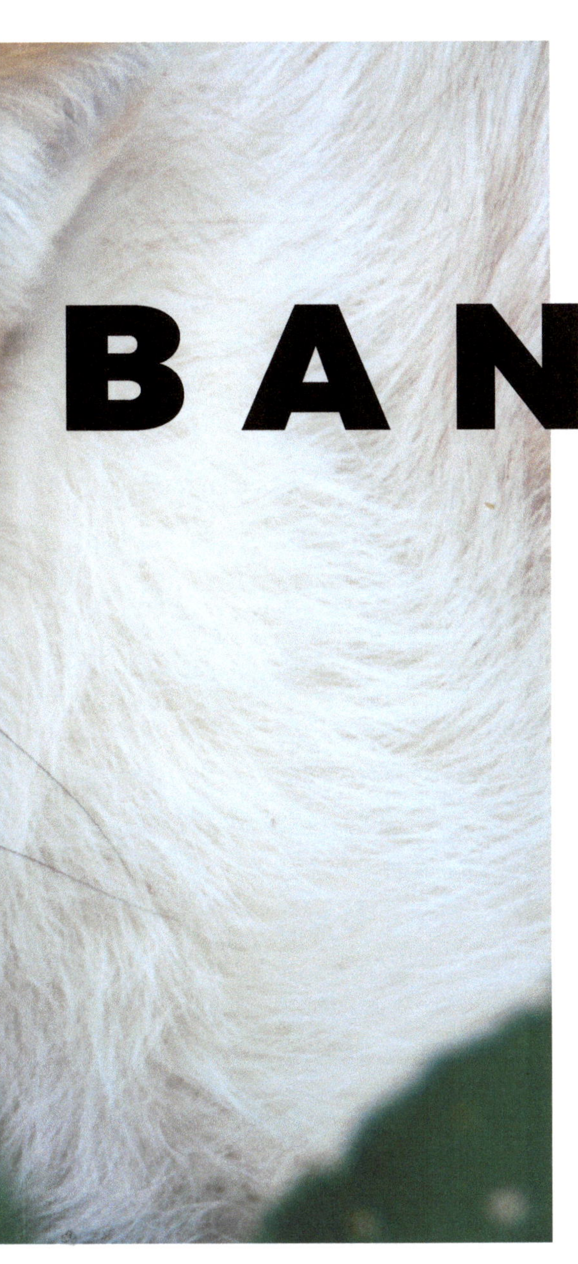

BANJO

THE
RED MARBLE
FOX

B A N J O was surrendered to Save a Fox when his owner could no longer keep him due to a family crisis. He was adopted into a new home in December 2018.

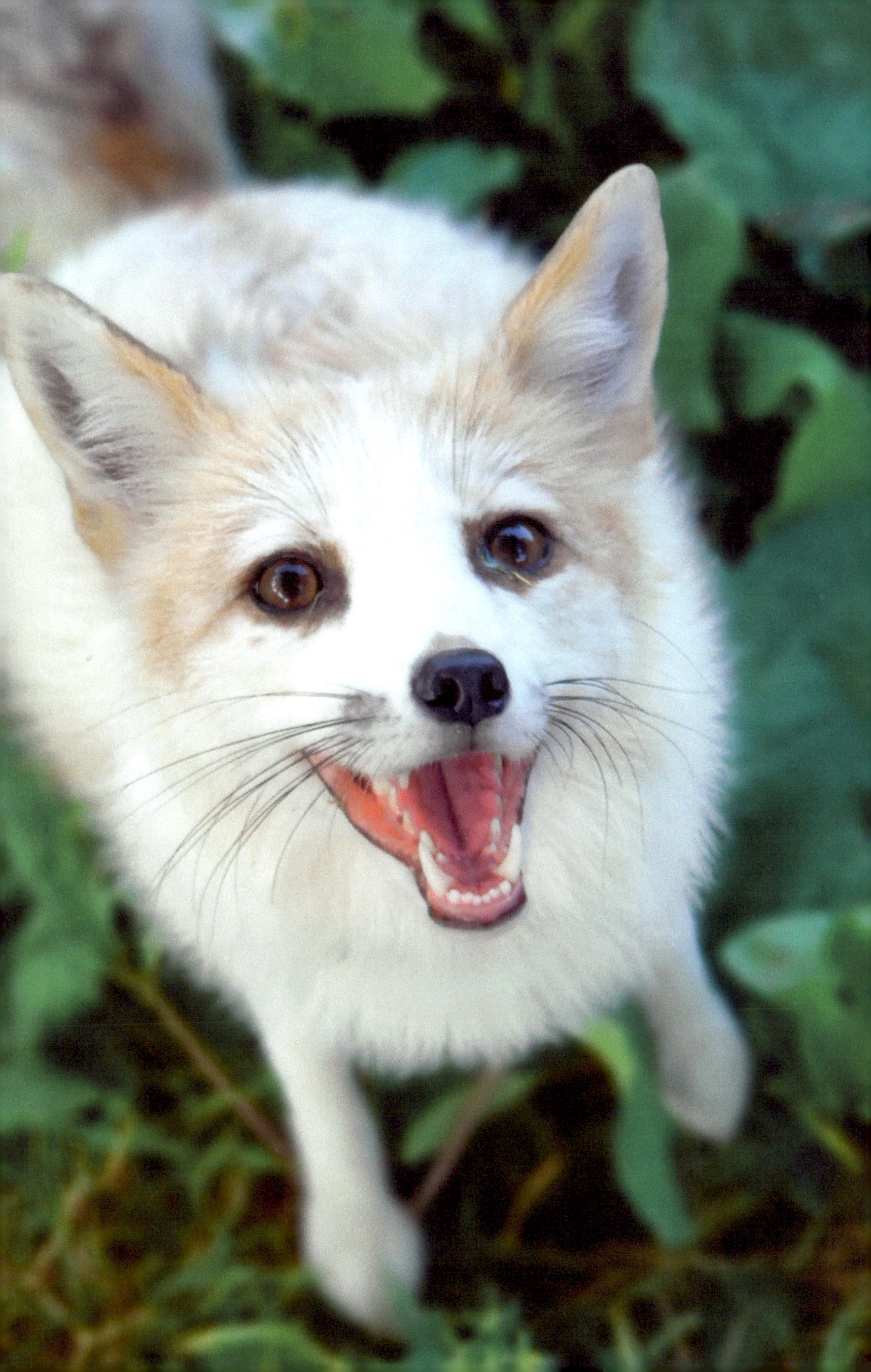

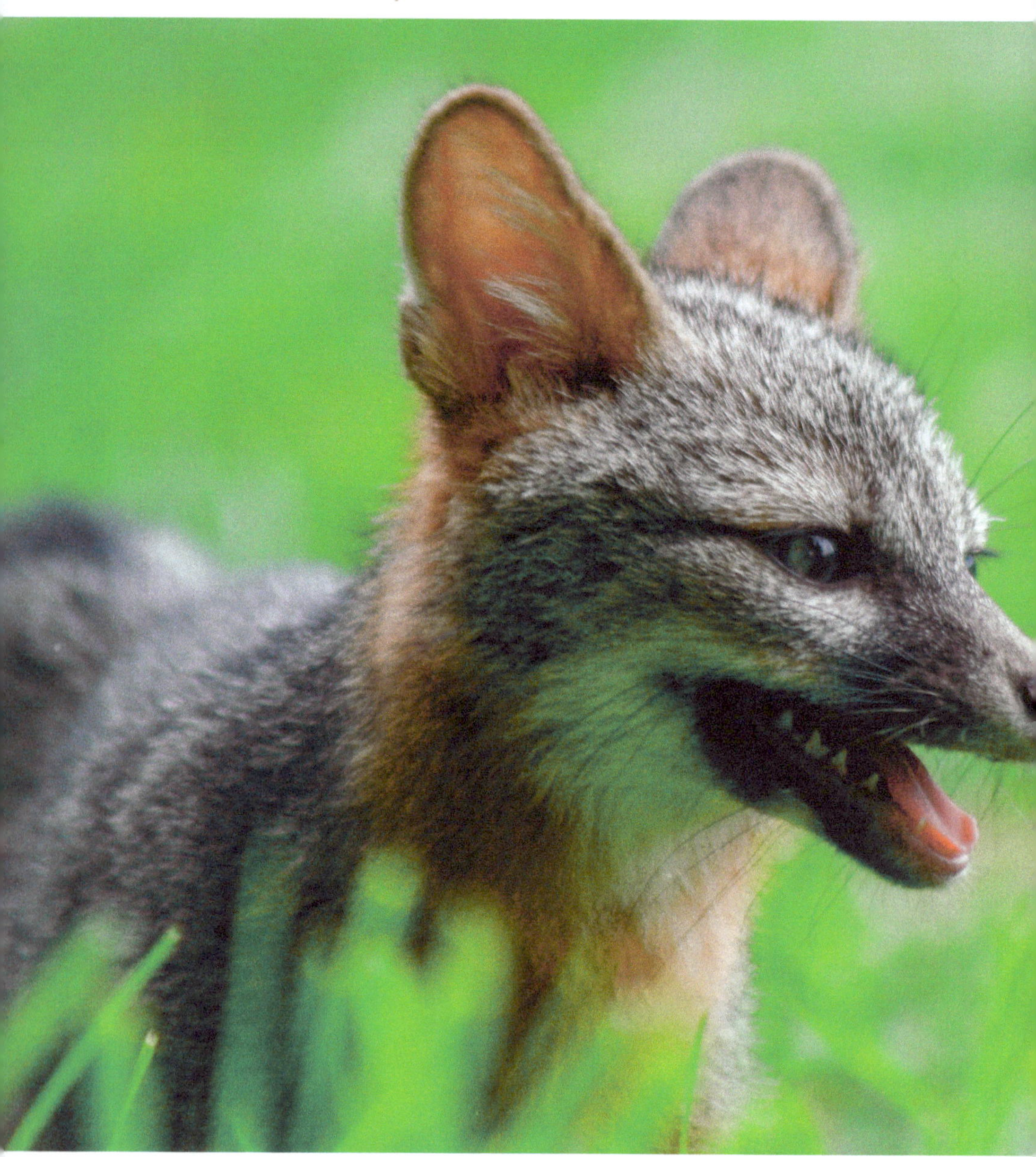

BATTY
Artemis
THE GRAY FOX

Batty Artemis and his litter were surrendered to Save a Fox in May 2019 by a pet fox breeder. The litter's mother had stopped nursing and properly caring for her kits when they were only a week old. Volunteers at the rescue raised and bottle-fed Batty and his two littermates until they were old enough to be adopted. Since Batty was so well-socialized and good with people Save a Fox decided that he should stay as a permanent resident at the rescue in order to be a fox ambassador for educational events. Batty traveled with Mikayla to Florida, socialized with guests at the rescue, and even appeared on local news in Minnesota.

Batty passed away tragically in August 2019, when he escaped the yard and was hit by a car just outside of the rescue. In his short life, Batty made an immense impact on Save a Fox, touching the lives of volunteers and fans around the world.

THE GRAY FOX is smaller than the red fox, weighing only 8–14 pounds. Native to North and Central America, gray foxes are avid tree-climbers who live in wooded areas. They are primarily nocturnal or crepuscular (active during dawn and twilight). Unlike the red fox, which comes in many coat colors when bred in captivity, the gray fox is very rarely found with any coloration besides its natural color: a distinctive red-and-gray body with a black tail tip.

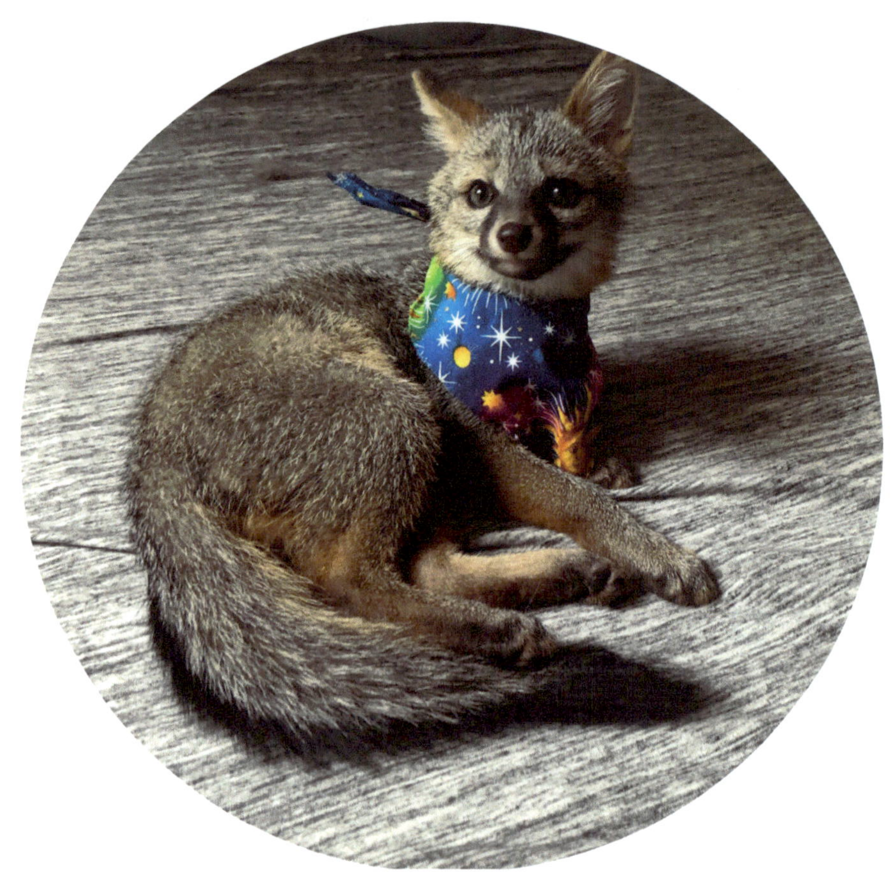

RIGHT PAGE: Batty rides in a front-carrier while on a trip to Florida. Batty accompanied Mikayla as the rescue's "fox ambassador" while the team visited potential locations for Save a Fox South—a second Save a Fox rescue location that's currently in the initial research and planning stage. To learn more about the plans for Save a Fox South or to donate to the new location's start-up, visit saveafox.org.

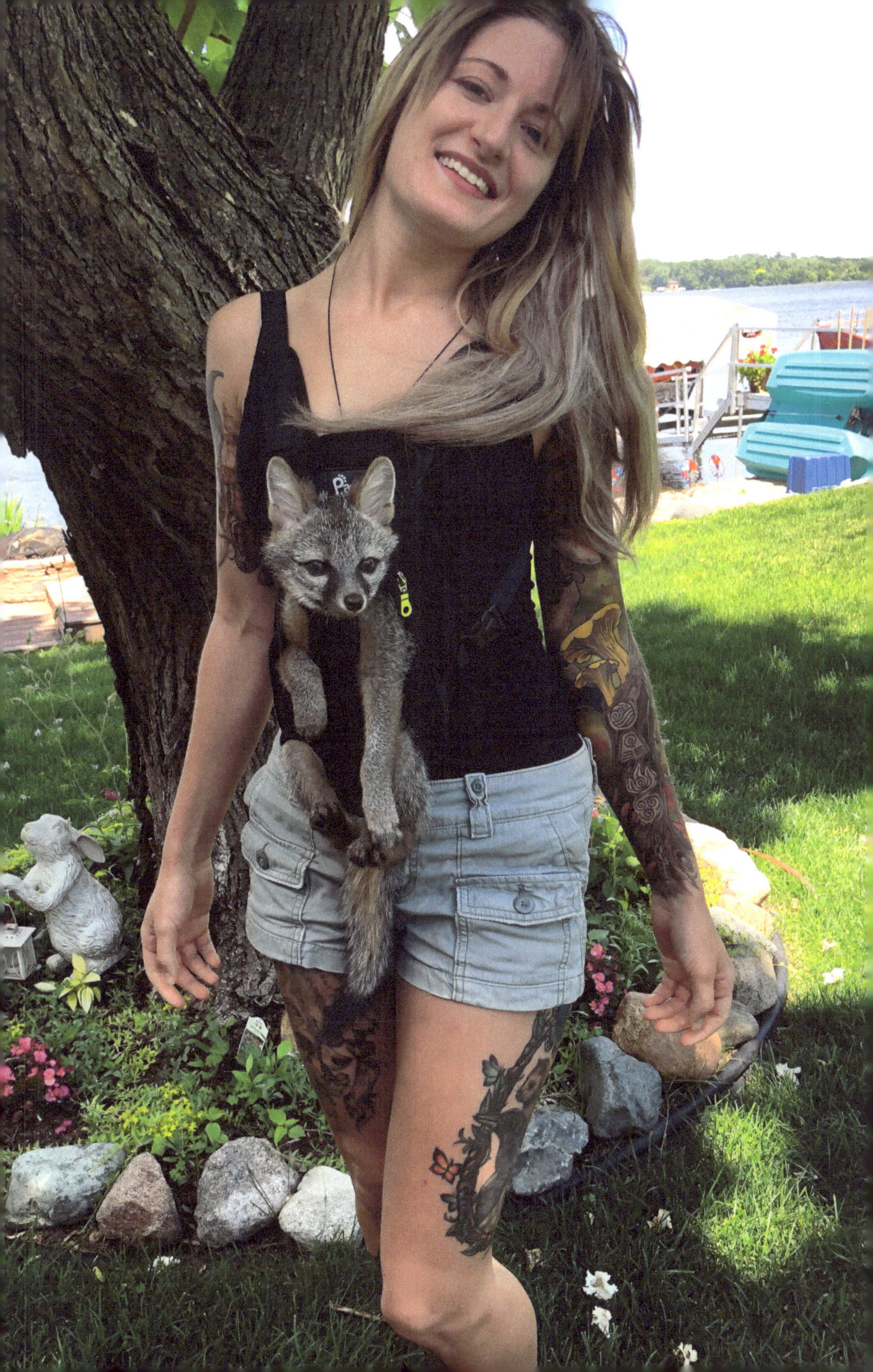

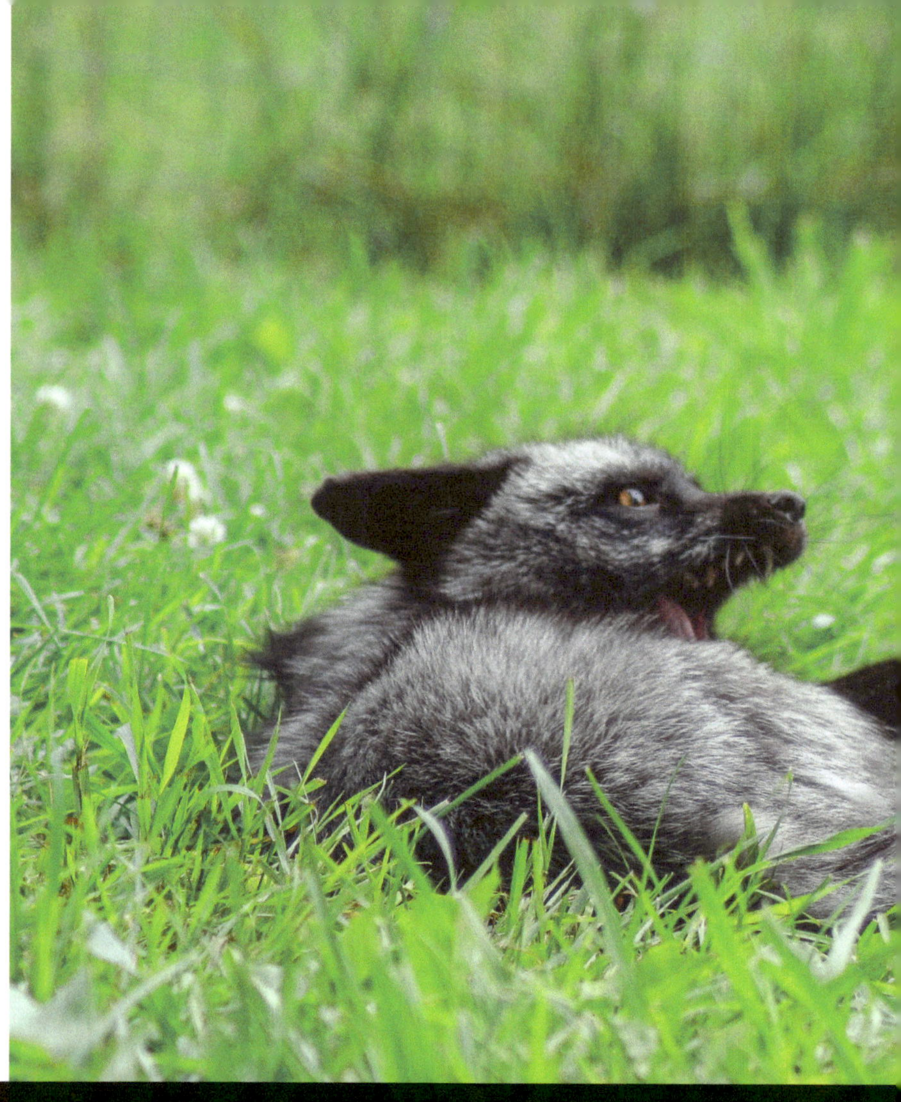

KELLIE KRUSE

Save a Fox volunteer

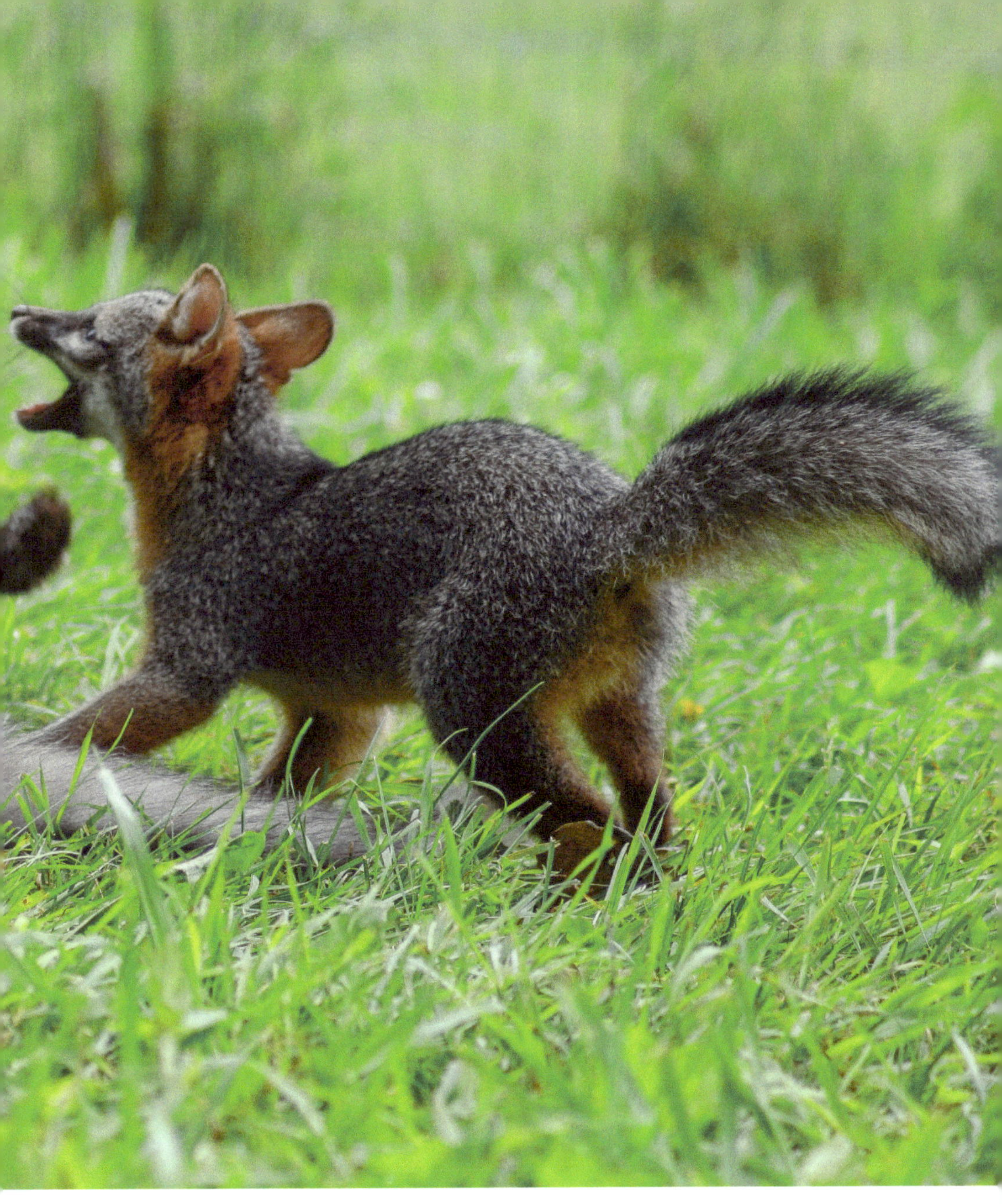

BATTY AND MUTTIAS wrestle in one of the fox yards. The two were inseparable friends at the rescue, and spent most of their time in the house together. Their friendship was special because, in the wild, gray foxes and red foxes are natural enemies. *Read Mutt's story on page 76.*

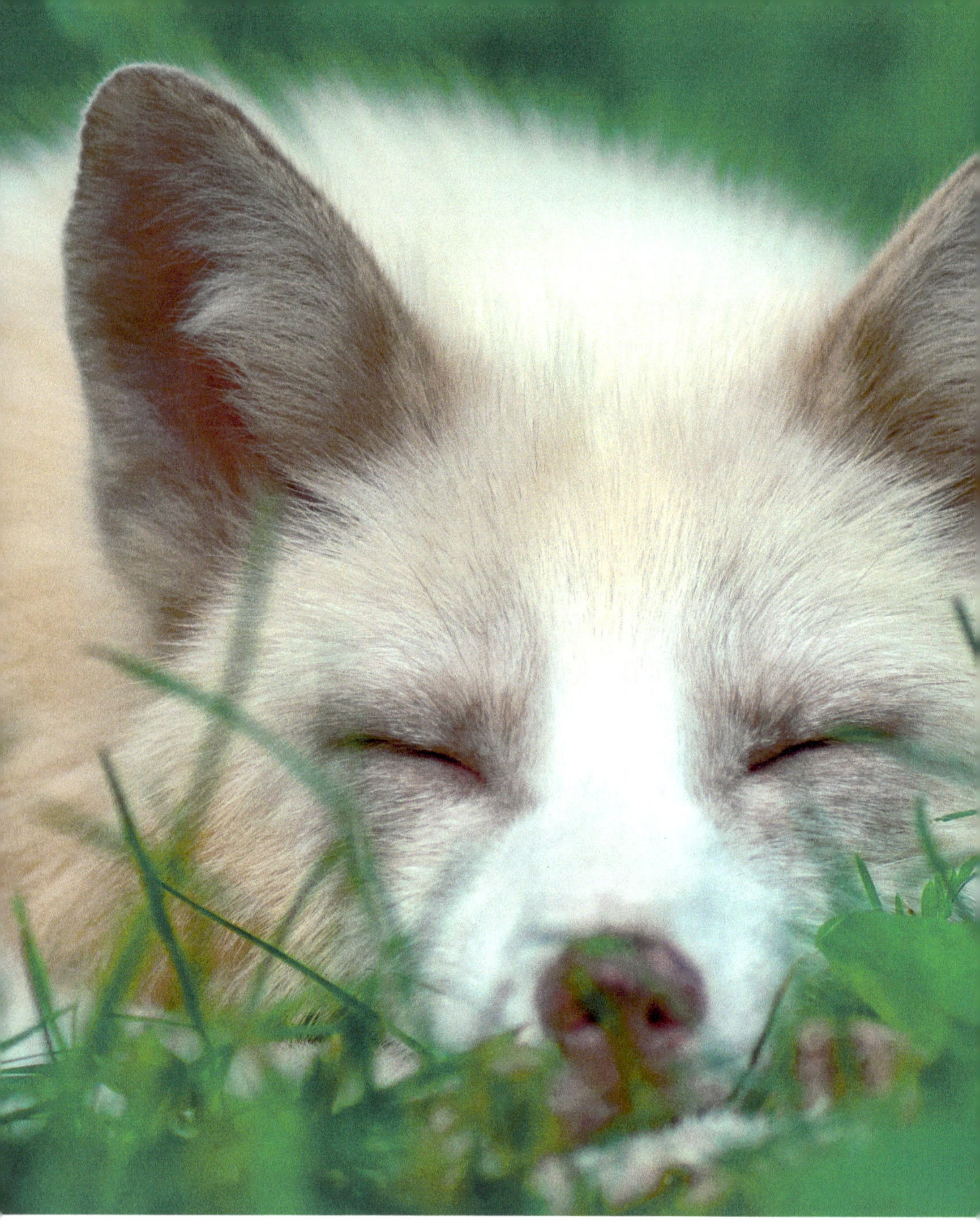

B O N G O was given to Save a Fox in March 2019 by a fur farmer after the fox grew too old to breed. Bongo was between 6 and 7 years old when he came to the rescue, making him the oldest fox at the sanctuary. After so many years in a cage, Bongo is now living life to the fullest, enjoying toy donations from sponsors and spending time with his friend and fellow fur farm rescue, Moby *(page 72)*. Bongo may be the father of another Save a Fox rescue, Rowyn. *Read Rowyn's story on page 86.*

BONGO

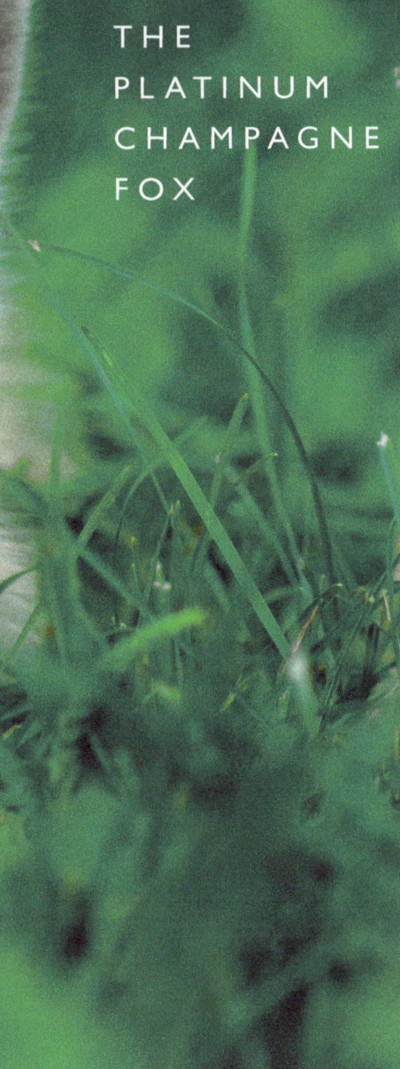

THE PLATINUM CHAMPAGNE FOX

> "
>
> Oh Bongo, you're so handsome. Did you know that Bongo is a fur farm rescue? In fact, he is the only fur farm rescue to have ever arrived with a name. He is the father (we believe) of Rowyn! The fur farmers that he came from had something akin to affection for him, and so when he was no longer going to be bred, they reached out to Mikayla at Save a Fox.
>
> **MERRI HAMPTON**
> *Rescue Coordinator at Save a Fox*
>
> "

THE PLATINUM CHAMPAGNE FOX has a very light, peach-hued coat. The "platinum" in its name means its coloring is lighter and more diluted than that of a regular champagne fox, and that it has white marks on the face, legs, belly, and chest. For an example of a champagne fox, see Rowyn's story on page 86.

Captain JACK

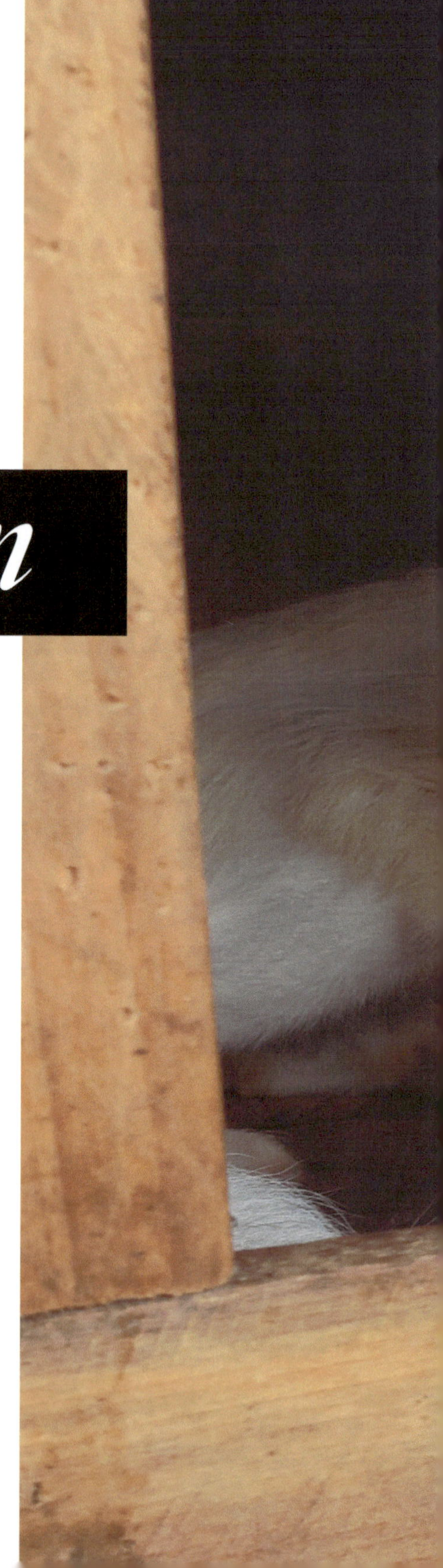

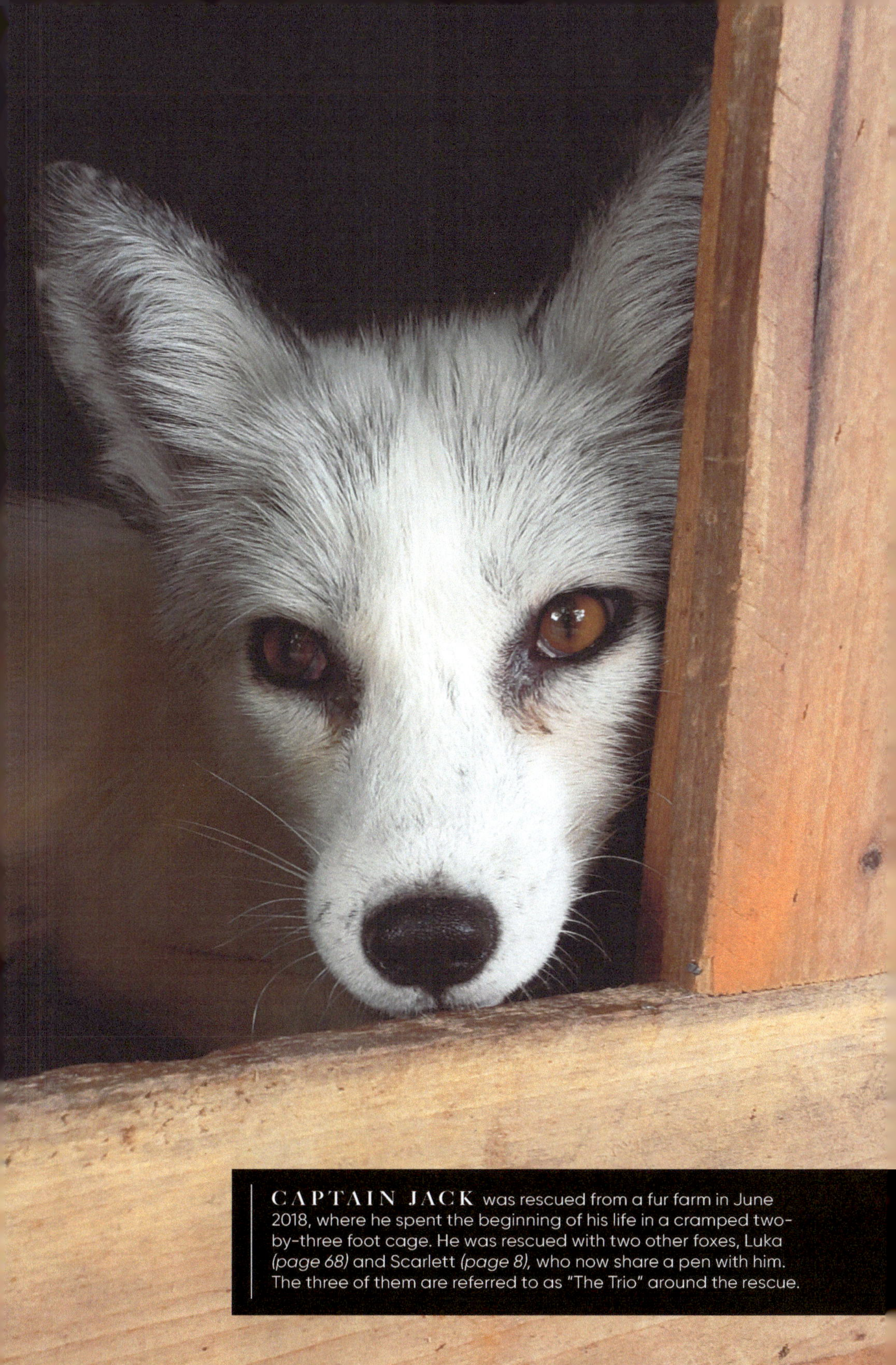

CAPTAIN JACK was rescued from a fur farm in June 2018, where he spent the beginning of his life in a cramped two-by-three foot cage. He was rescued with two other foxes, Luka *(page 68)* and Scarlett *(page 8)*, who now share a pen with him. The three of them are referred to as "The Trio" around the rescue.

DIXIE
DIXIE
DIXIE-DO

THE RED FOX

DIXIE
DIXIE
DIXIE

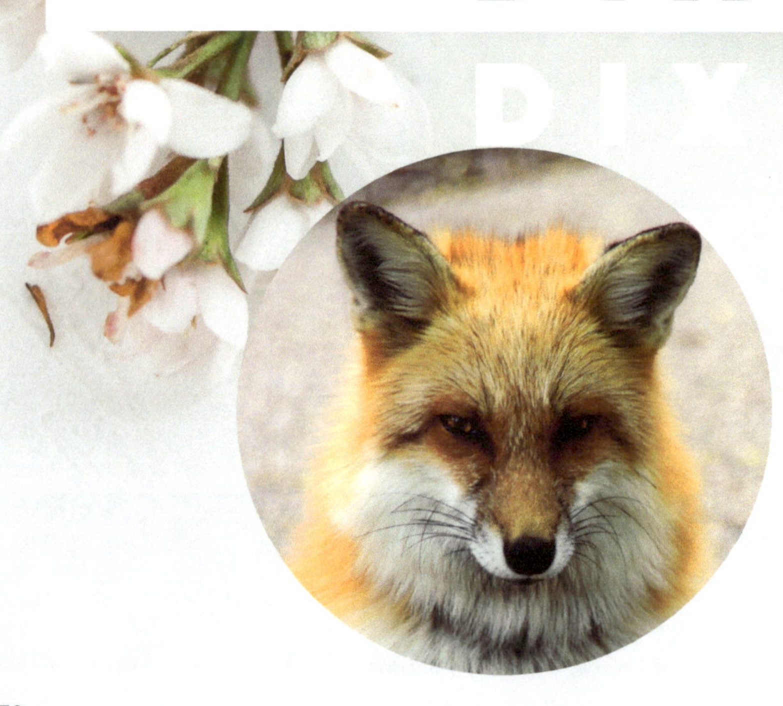

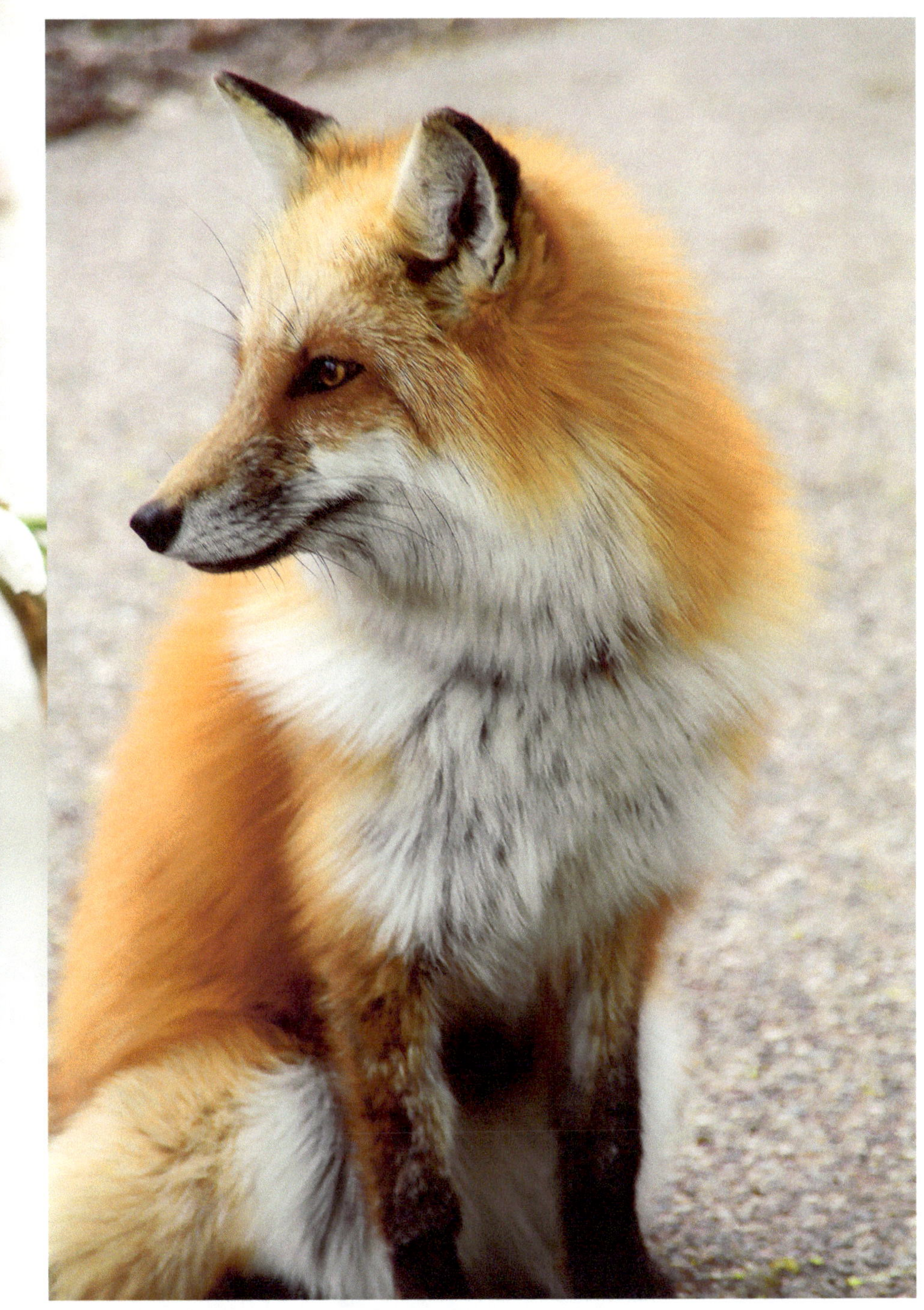

DIXIE came to the rescue in 2017 after her owner passed away unexpectedly. She was adopted by Mikayla Raines in October 2018, and is now a permanent resident of Save a Fox.

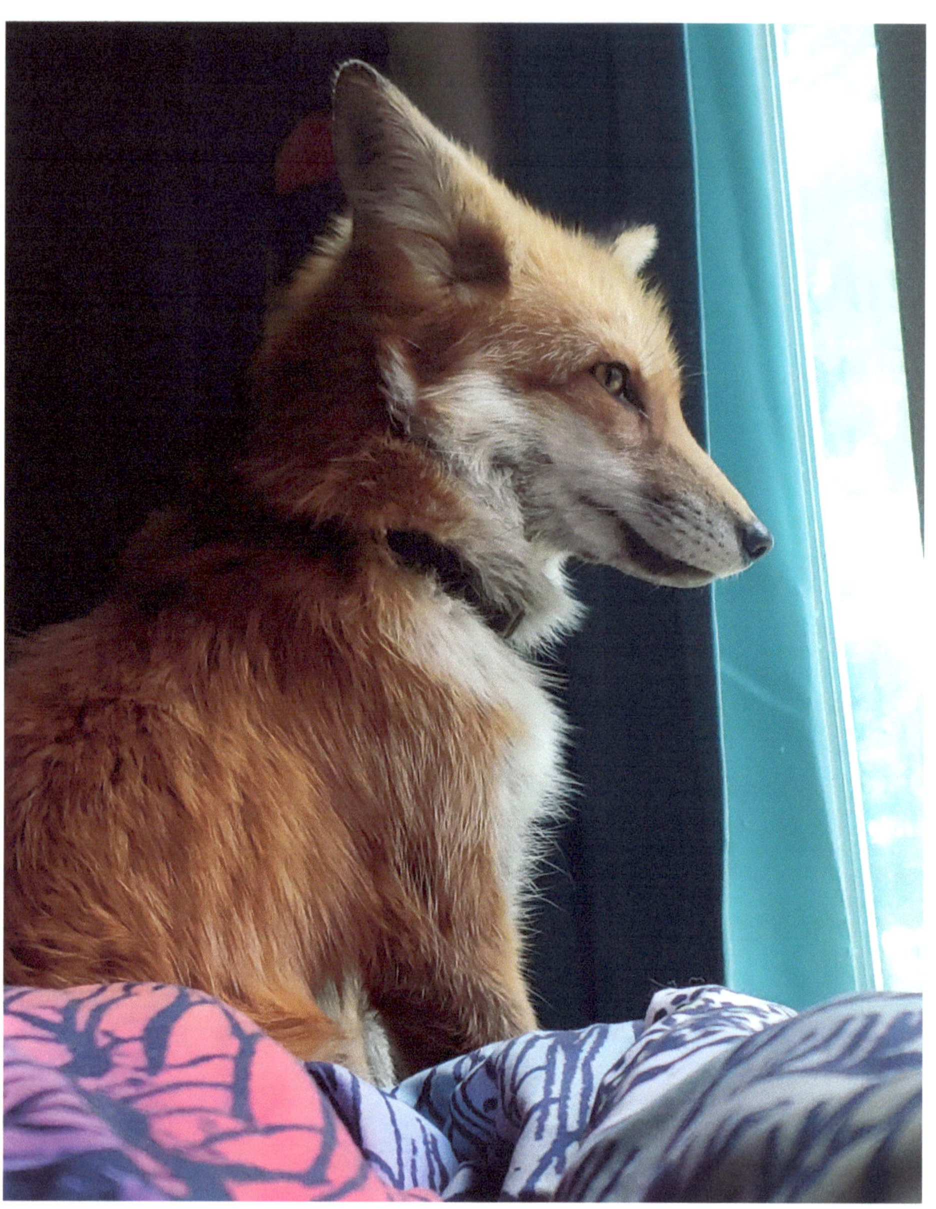

MIKAYLA RAINES
Owner of Save a Fox

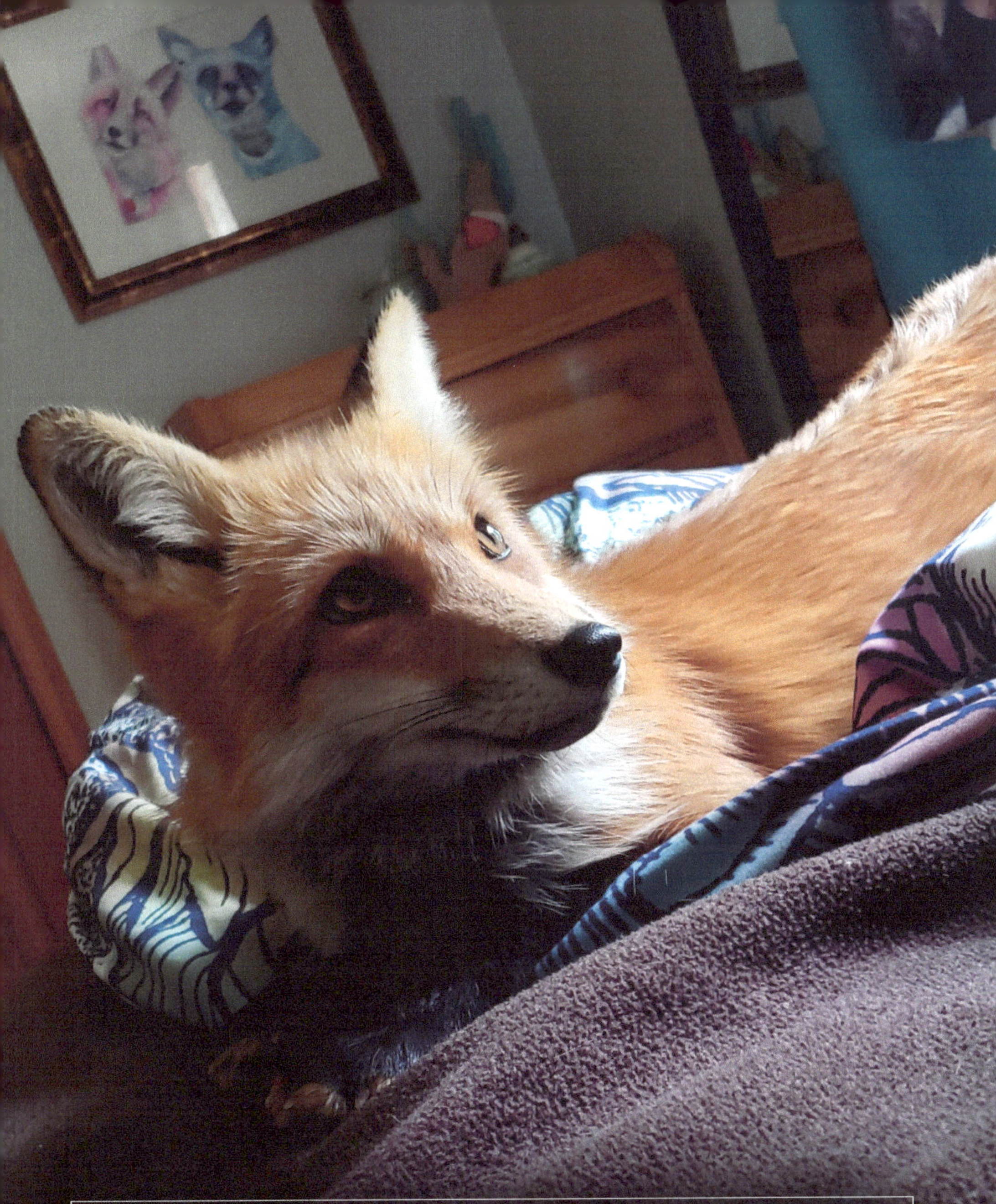

THE RED FOX is the most common fox species in the world. It can be found all throughout the Northern Hemisphere, including North America, Europe, Asia, northern Africa, and it has even been introduced to Australia. The red fox is extremely adaptable to different habitats. It can comfortably live in forests, mountains, deserts, grasslands, and suburban areas. Most of the foxes at Save a Fox are actually red foxes, despite their vastly different appearances. Around 100 color variations of the red fox exist, the majority of which are the result of selective breeding in captivity.

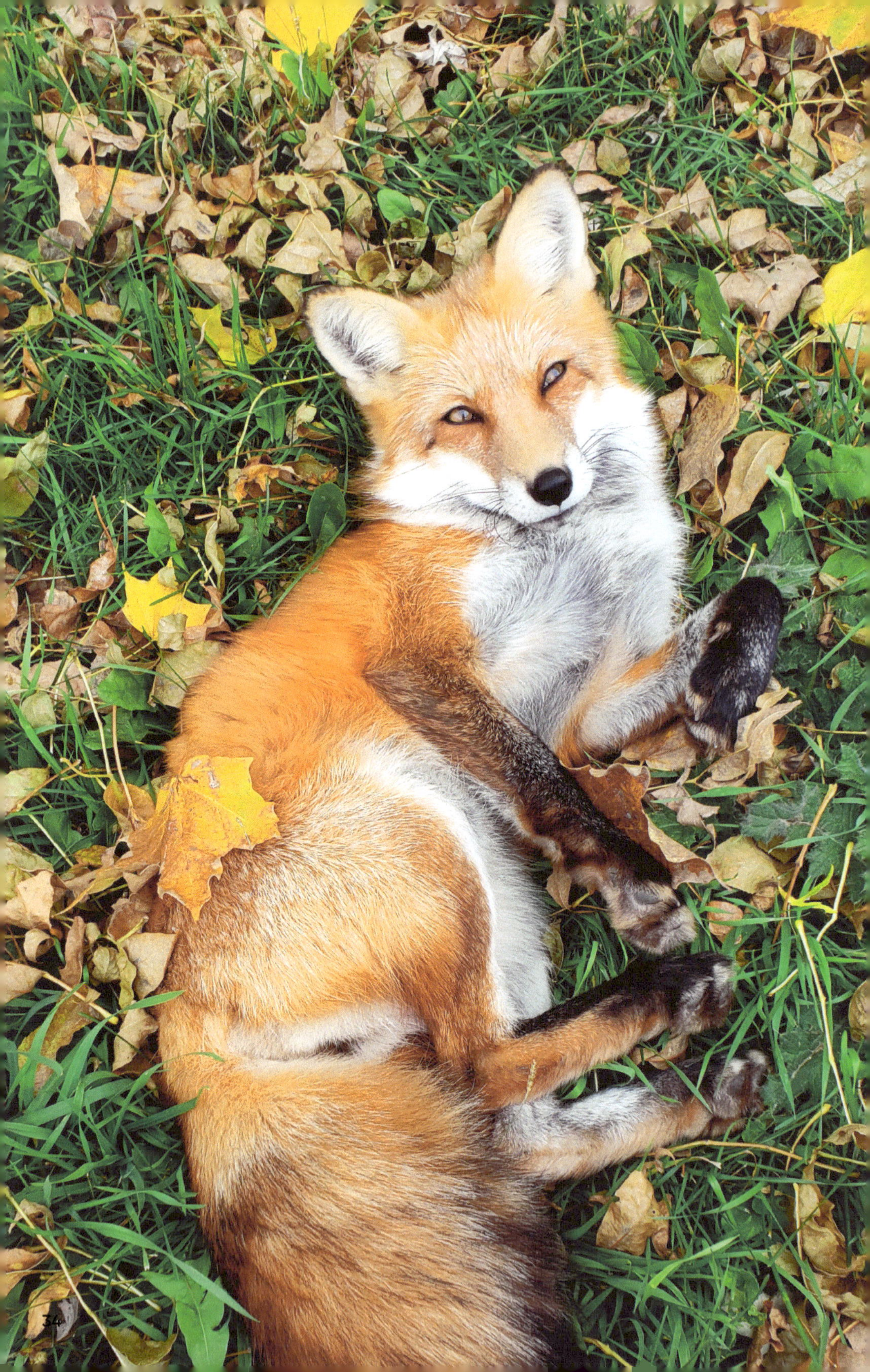

"

Dixie is full of personality. In the spring, we introduce all of our weaned kits to Dixie. She acts as a great role model for them. They dig dens and run together. During this time, she's a mom with a mission, and won't tolerate human interaction as often.

Most of our kits have already been adopted this year—there are only three left. Each time one leaves, I am a little heartbroken, because bonding with the little ones is an incomparable experience. But it is also nice to get Dixie's flirtatious little attitude back.

MIKAYLA RAINES
Owner of Save a Fox

(Written in September 2018)

"

So excited to be sponsoring this gorgeous girl! She was saved from a fur farm where she was going to be killed due to a genetic mutation that changes the texture of her coat. She's missing her guard hairs, which makes her 'undesirable' in the fur world. I think she's perfect, and I'm so glad she's learning how to trust people and how to live freely, like every fox deserves.

LILY HANSON
Duchess's sponsor

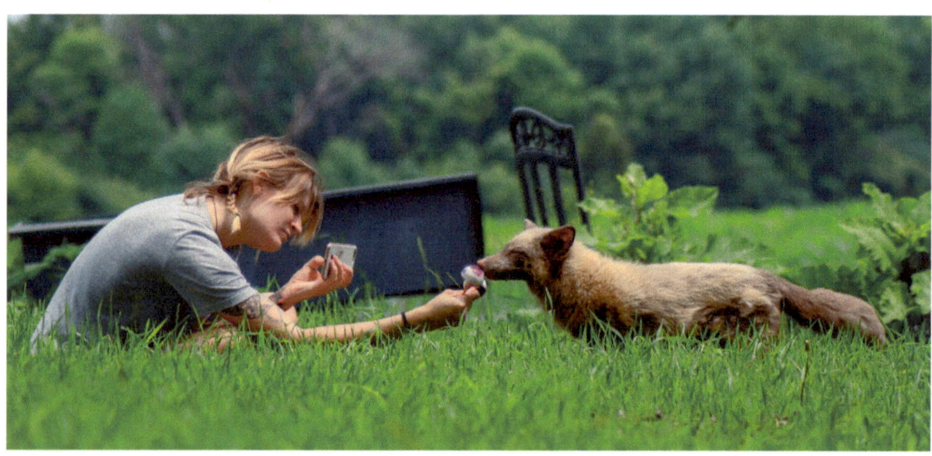

DUCHESS was rescued from a fur farm in January 2019. She is missing her guard hairs, which are long, coarse hairs that protect an animal's shorter, softer undercoat. Without her guard hairs, Duchess's pelt was not desirable to fur farmers. She was scheduled to be killed, but Save a Fox stepped in and rescued her. Above, Mikayla snaps a photo of Duchess eating a "foxicle"—a fruity frozen treat that keeps the foxes cool on hot summer days.

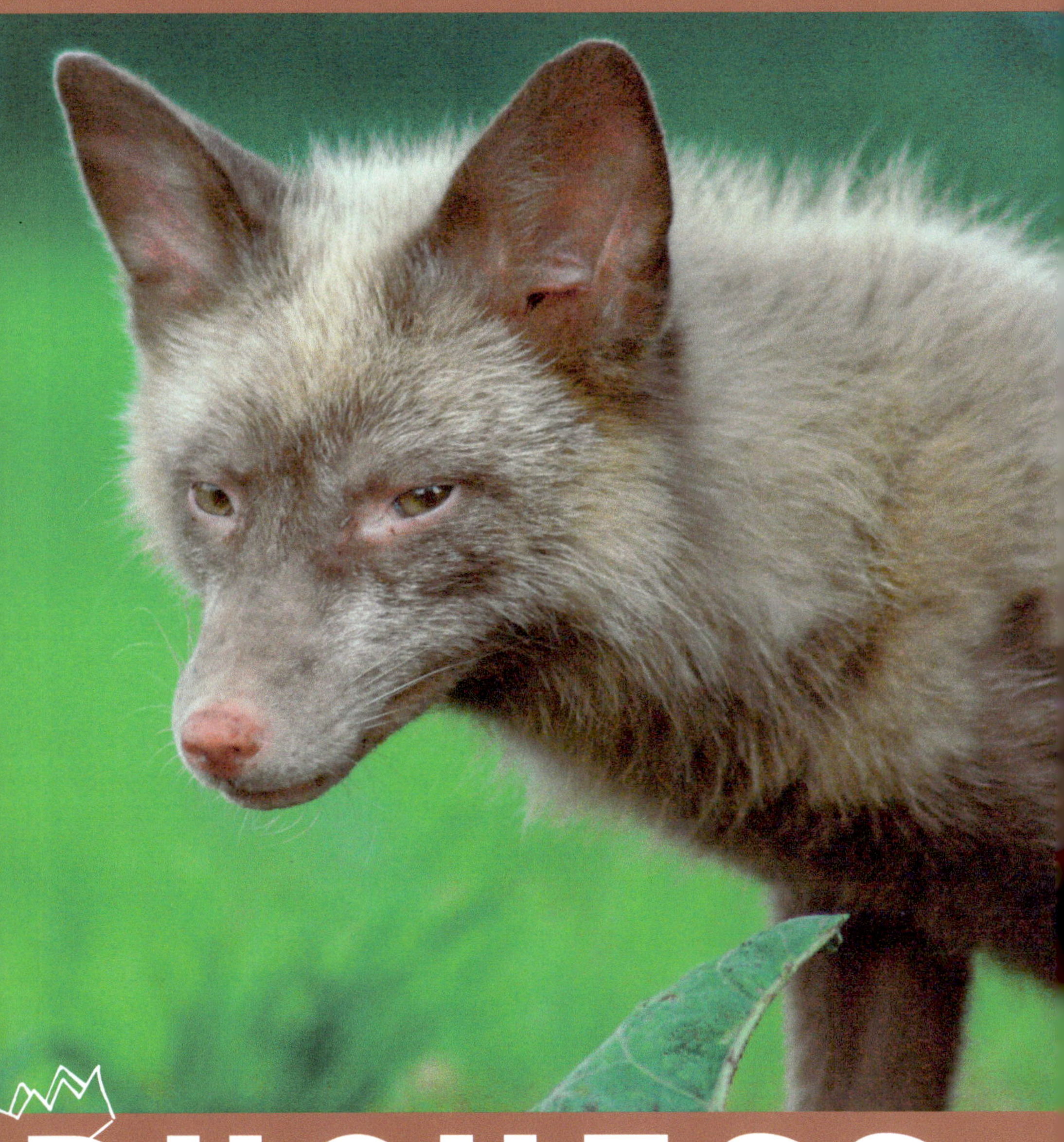

DUCHESS

THE DARK CHAMPAGNE FOX

THE DARK CHAMPAGNE FOX is a darker variation of the champagne fox, which is also called the "pink fox" or "pink champagne fox." Champagne foxes are popular in the pet trade. To see an example of a regular champagne fox, see Rowyn on page 86.

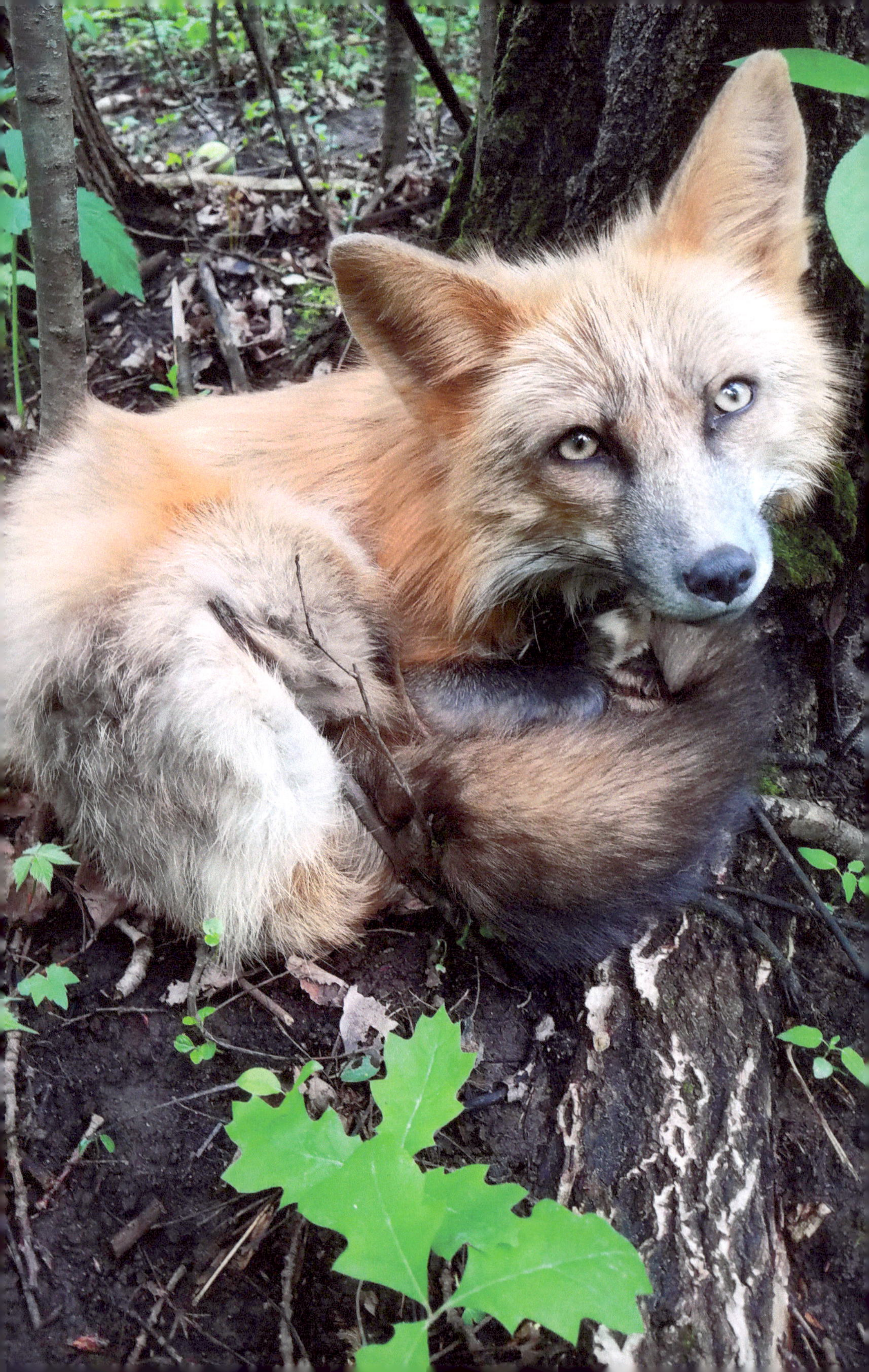

Farrah Foxett

THE DAKOTA GOLD FOX

Farrah Foxett was a tiny, one-week-old kit when a domestic fox breeder surrendered her to Mikayla Raines in 2015. Farrah was suffering from a life-threatening upper respiratory infection and required around-the-clock care. Mikayla stayed up for three suspenseful nights bottle feeding her until her condition finally stabilized. Since Farrah was bred in captivity to be a pet, she did not have the instincts she would need to survive in the wild. So, Mikayla adopted and raised Farrah as her personal pet fox, and the two became inseparable.

Farrah passed away tragically and unexpectedly on October 8, 2017. Farrah was one of Mikayla's first fox rescues, and her short but joyful life played a large role in inspiring the beginnings of Save a Fox rescue.

THE DAKOTA GOLD FOX, also known as the pearl gold fox, is one of approximately 100 color variations of the red fox that have been developed through selective breeding. Dakota golds are distinguished by their pale orange bodies and gray feet, ears, and tail.

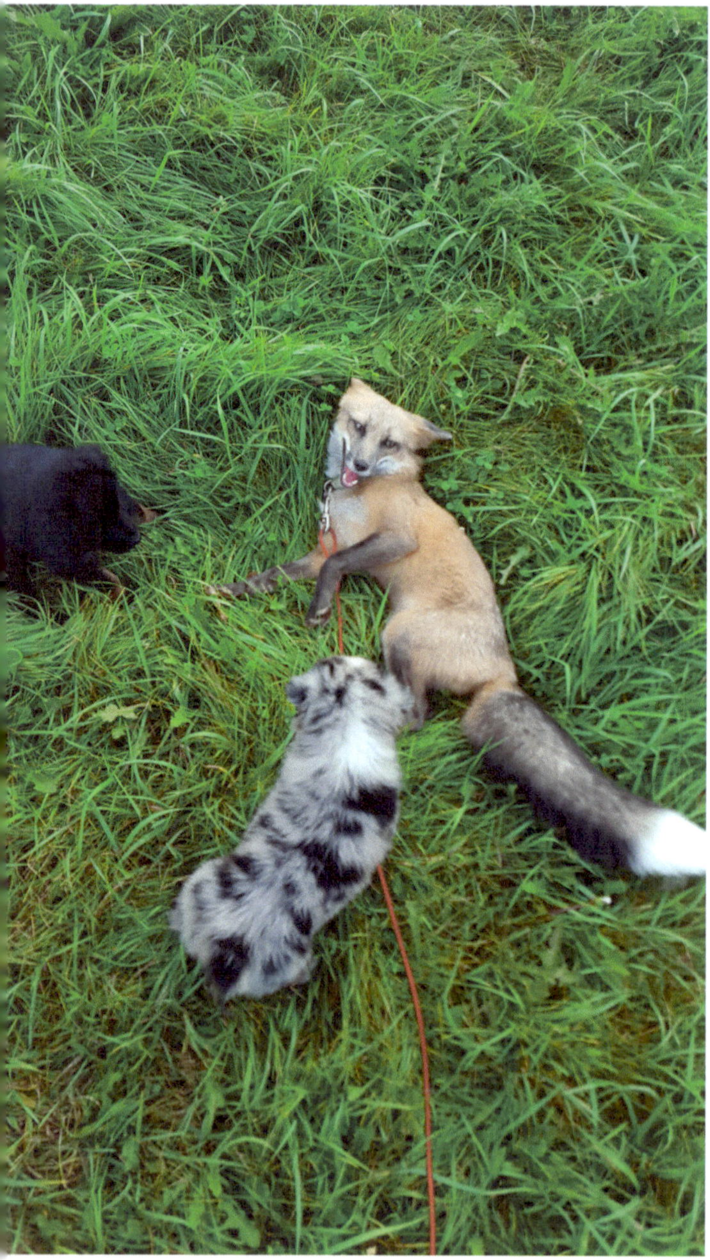

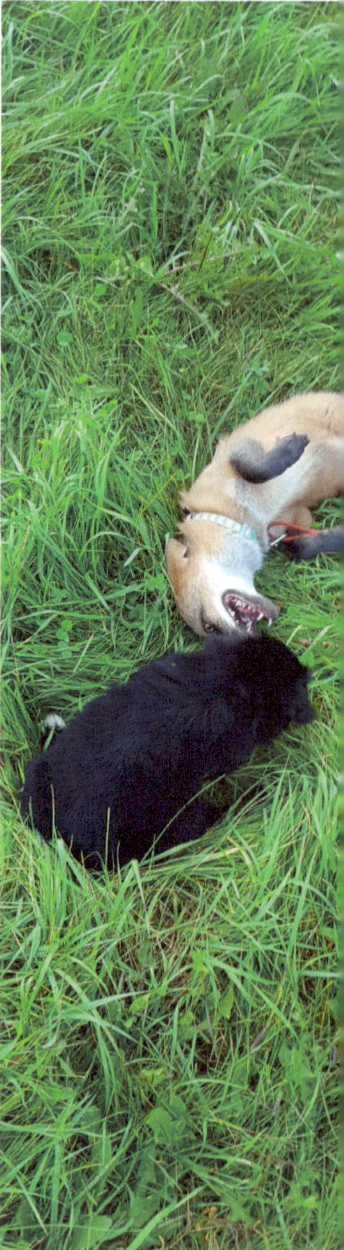

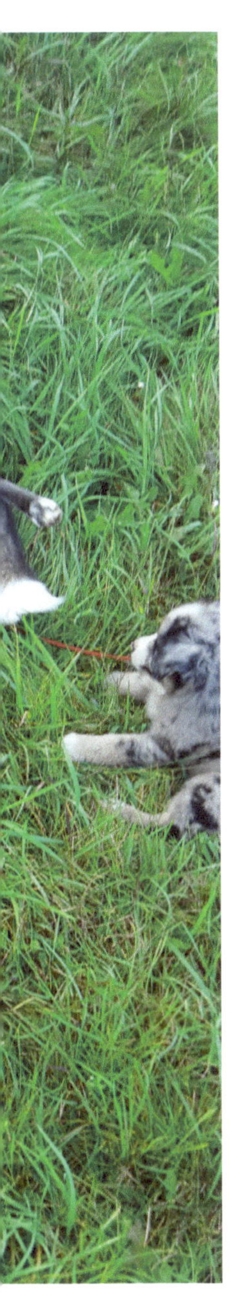

> **66** Farrah Foxett says, **99**
> 'Please, please, can we
> keep the puppies?!'

MIKAYLA RAINES
Owner of Save a Fox

FARRAH FOXETT acted as a mother to many of the fox kits who came to the rescue. In the wild, it's not uncommon for female foxes who don't have kits to act as "nannies" and help raise other females' kits. Farrah extended this motherly love to puppies, too! In these photos, Farrah plays with two Australian Shepherd puppies who came through the rescue.

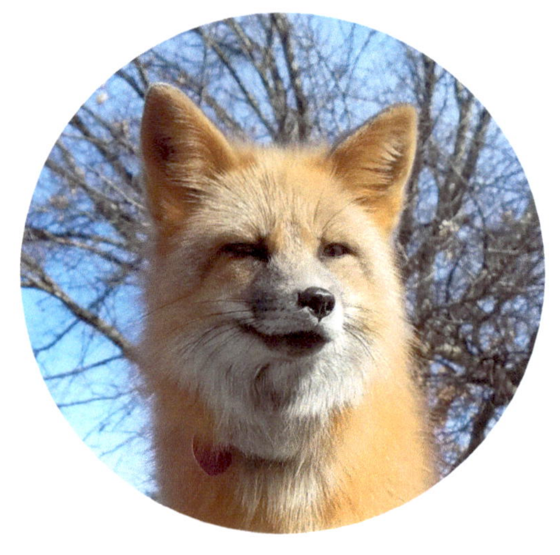

> **She thinks she is a tree fox. She climbs everything!**

MIKAYLA RAINES
Owner of Save a Fox

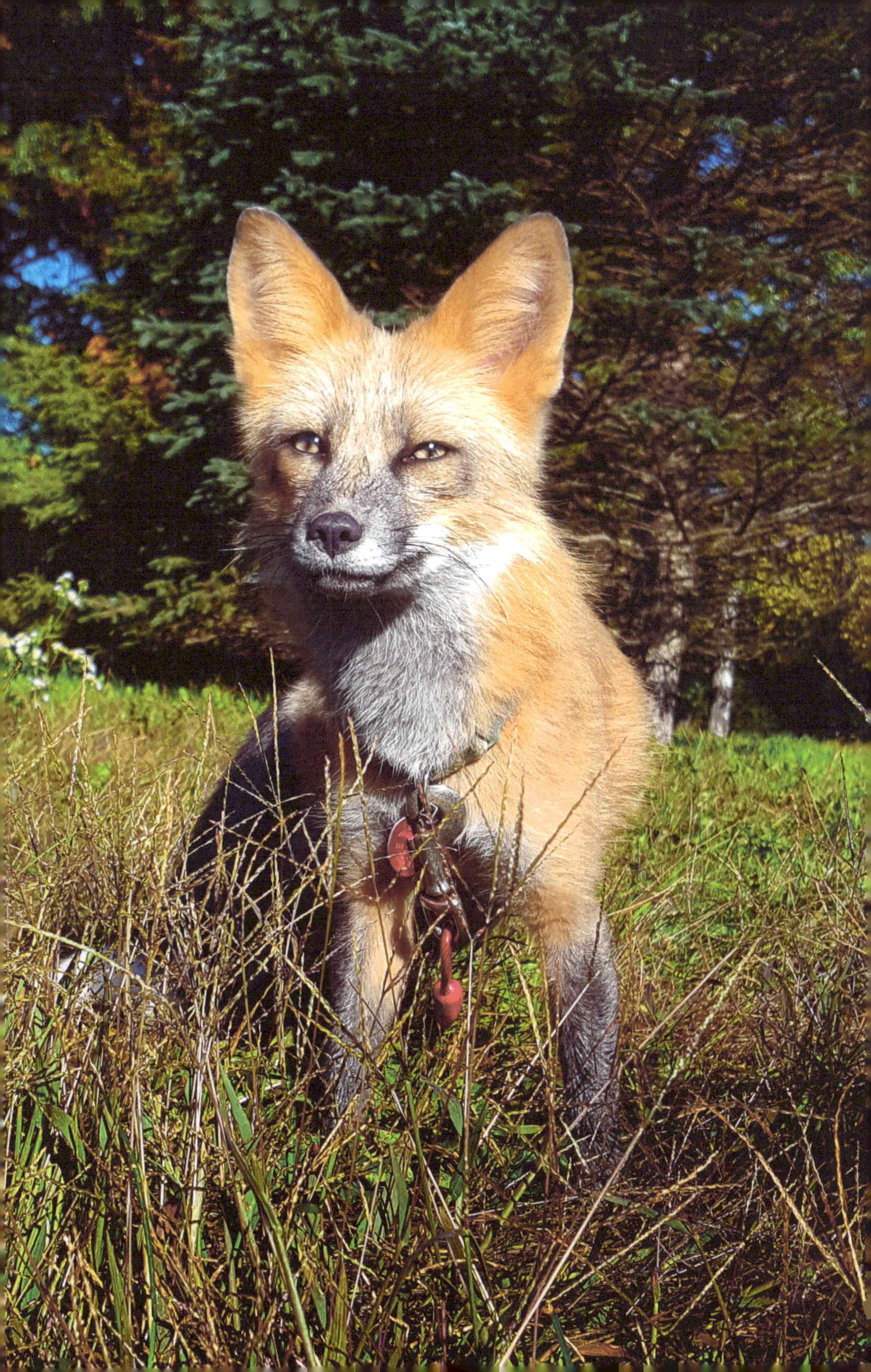

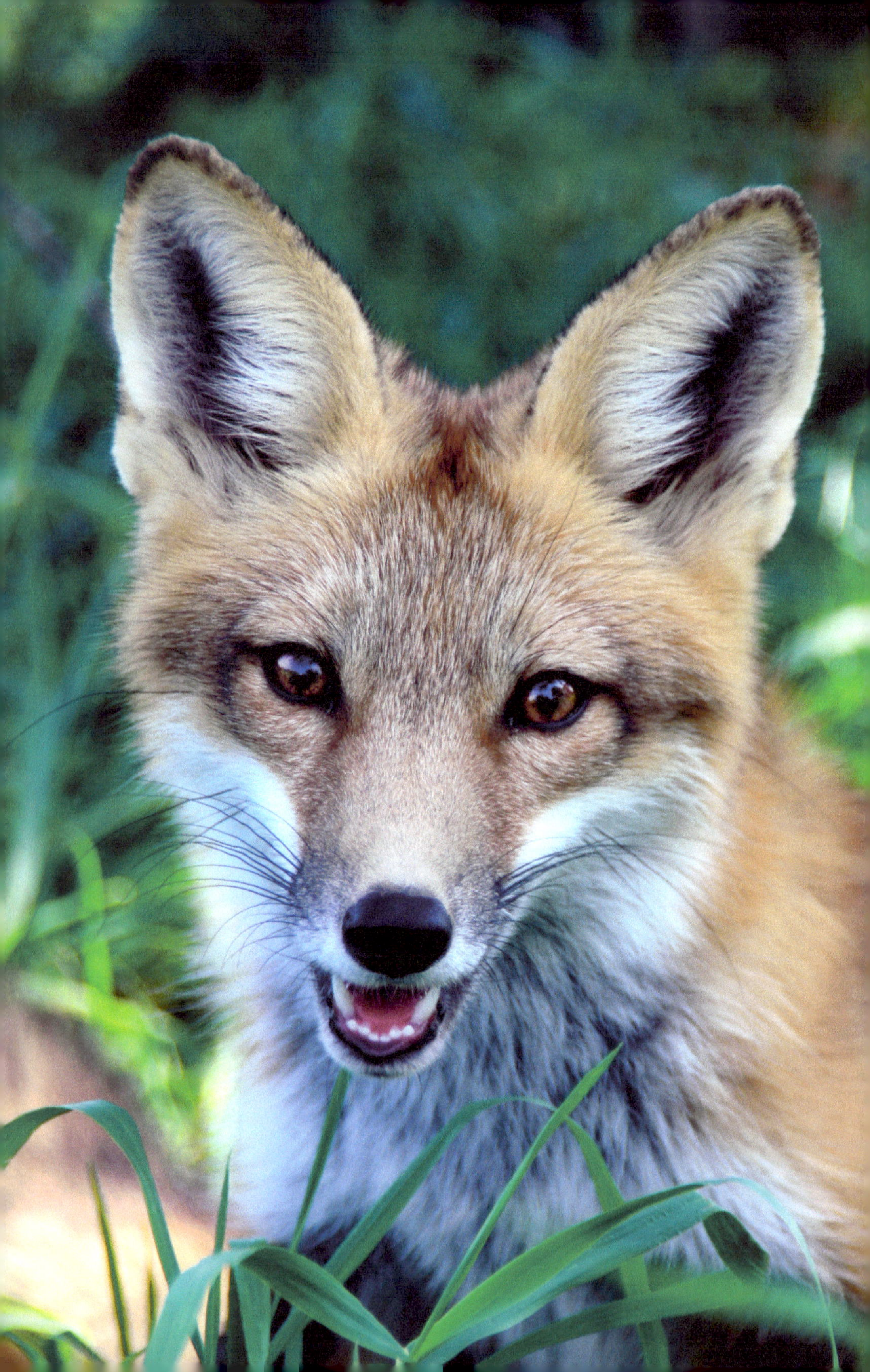

FELIX

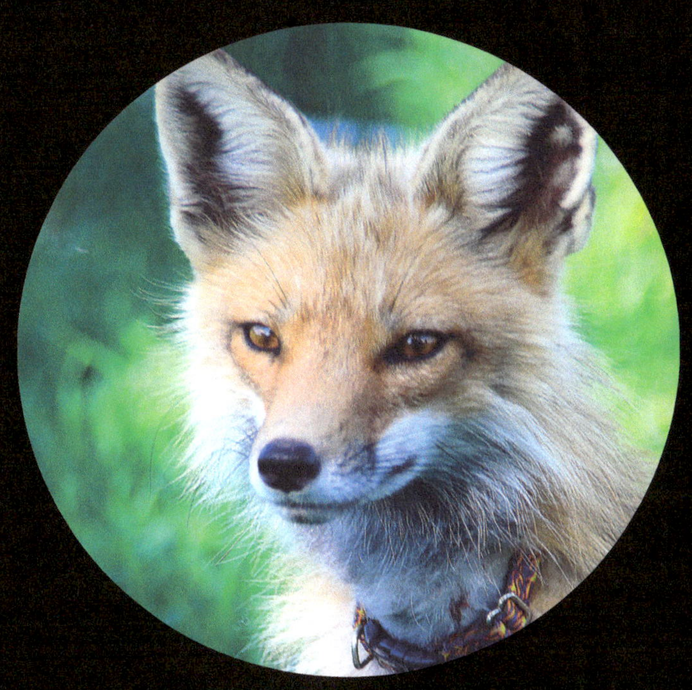

THE RED FOX

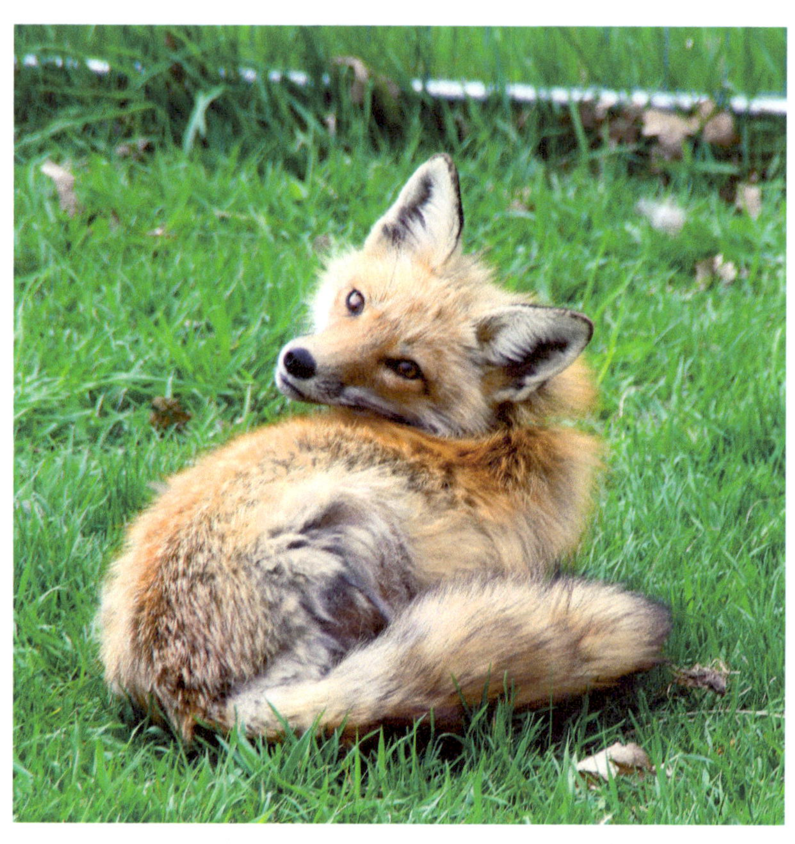

Finally a Felix sighting! We like to call him our 'wild fox' because he never shows himself to visitors and is almost impossible to get photos of.

MIKAYLA RAINES
Owner of Save a Fox

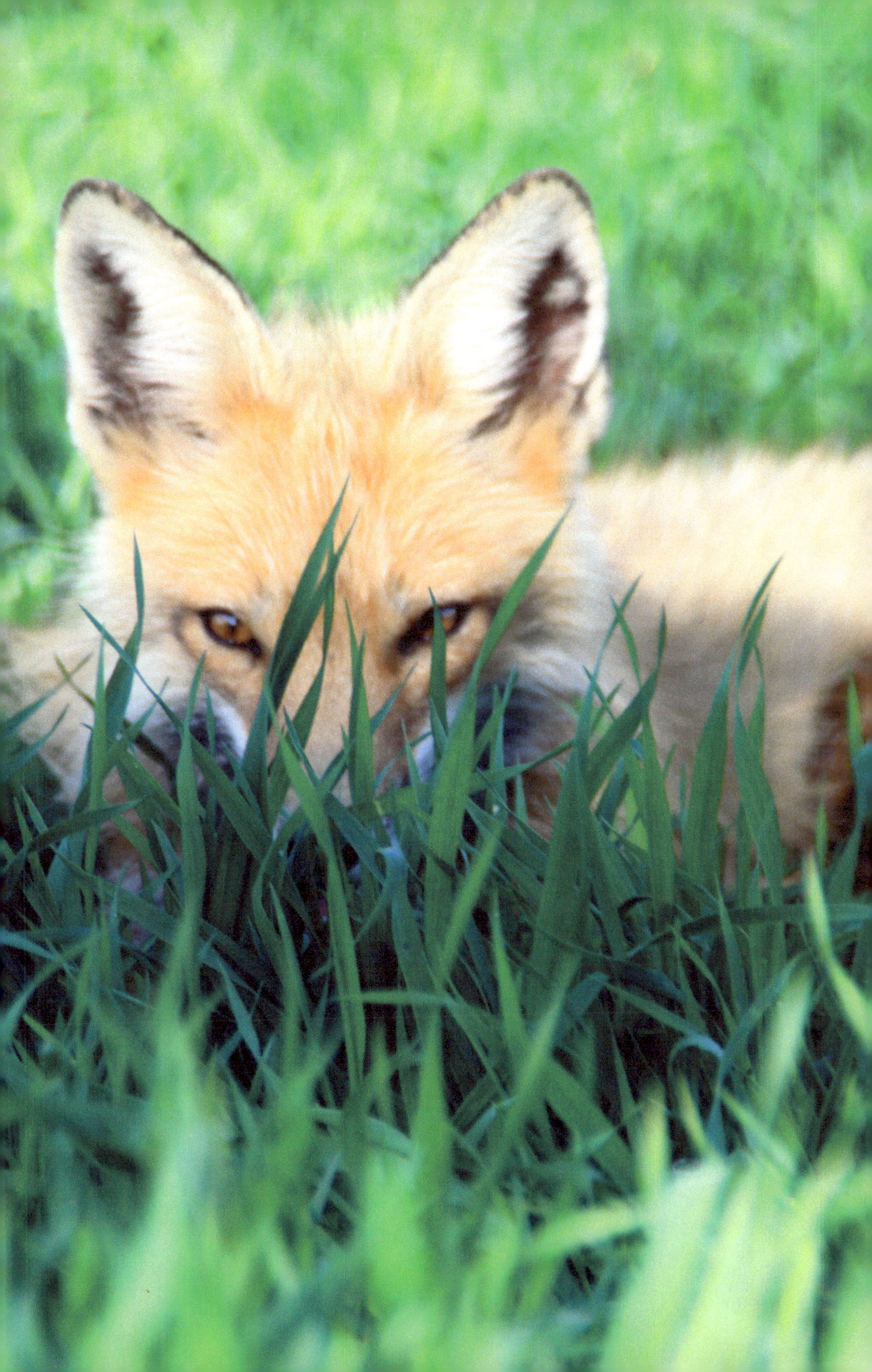

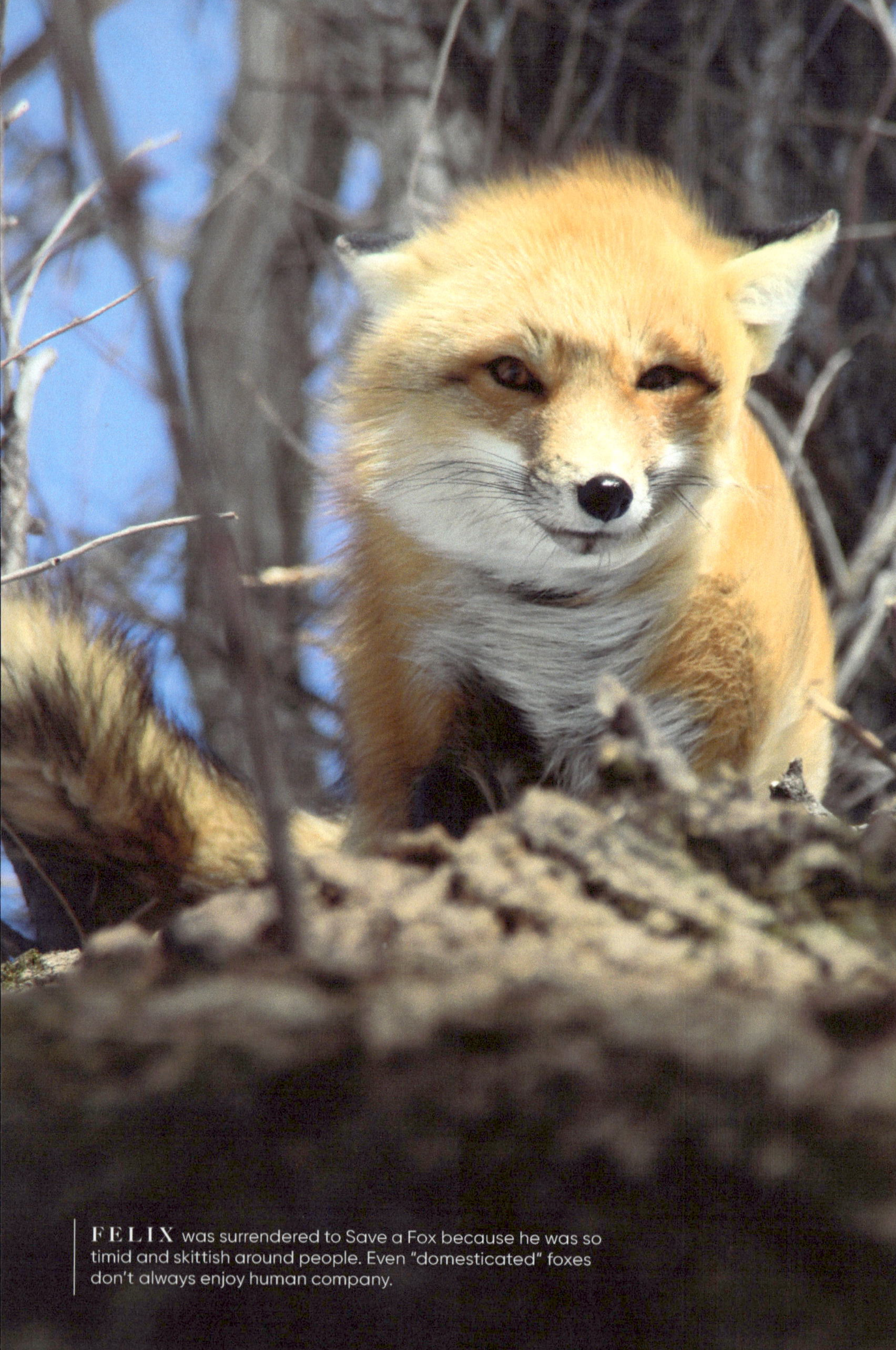

FELIX was surrendered to Save a Fox because he was so timid and skittish around people. Even "domesticated" foxes don't always enjoy human company.

" Felix, the elusive tree fox. "

KIM DAVIS
Photographer and Save a Fox volunteer

Fig

THE DAKOTA GOLD FOX

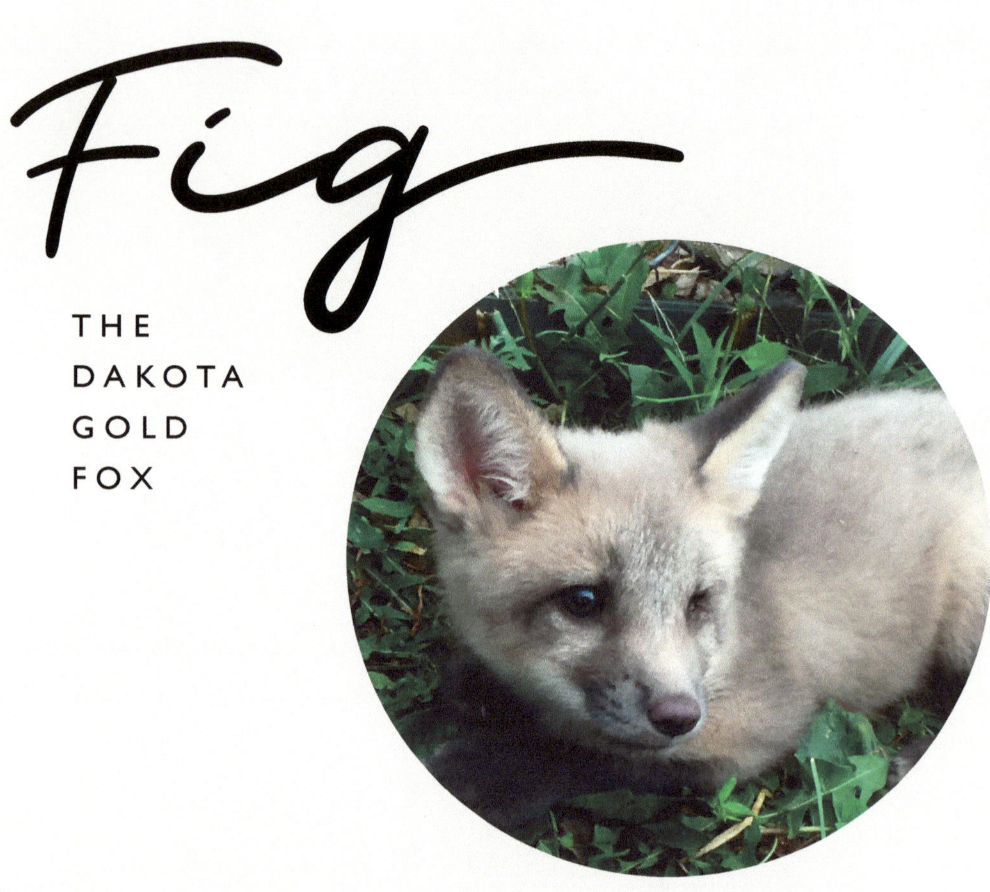

FIG was born on a fur farm in the spring of 2017. When he was very young, he was cut on his wire cage and contracted a bacterial infection, which blinded him in his left eye and caused him to lose his right foot and most of his toes. With the help of dedicated Save a Fox volunteers, Fig was nursed back to health. He was adopted in June 2017 by the owner of the widely-popular @juniperfoxx on Instagram, and has gained millions of fans around the world. When Fig first arrived at his new home, he was skittish and wary of humans, but now he is a confident and smiling young adult fox who loves his big sister, Juniper, and little brother, Elmwood. Fig's wounds have fully healed, and he wears a custom-made prosthetic leg to help pad his wrist while he walks.

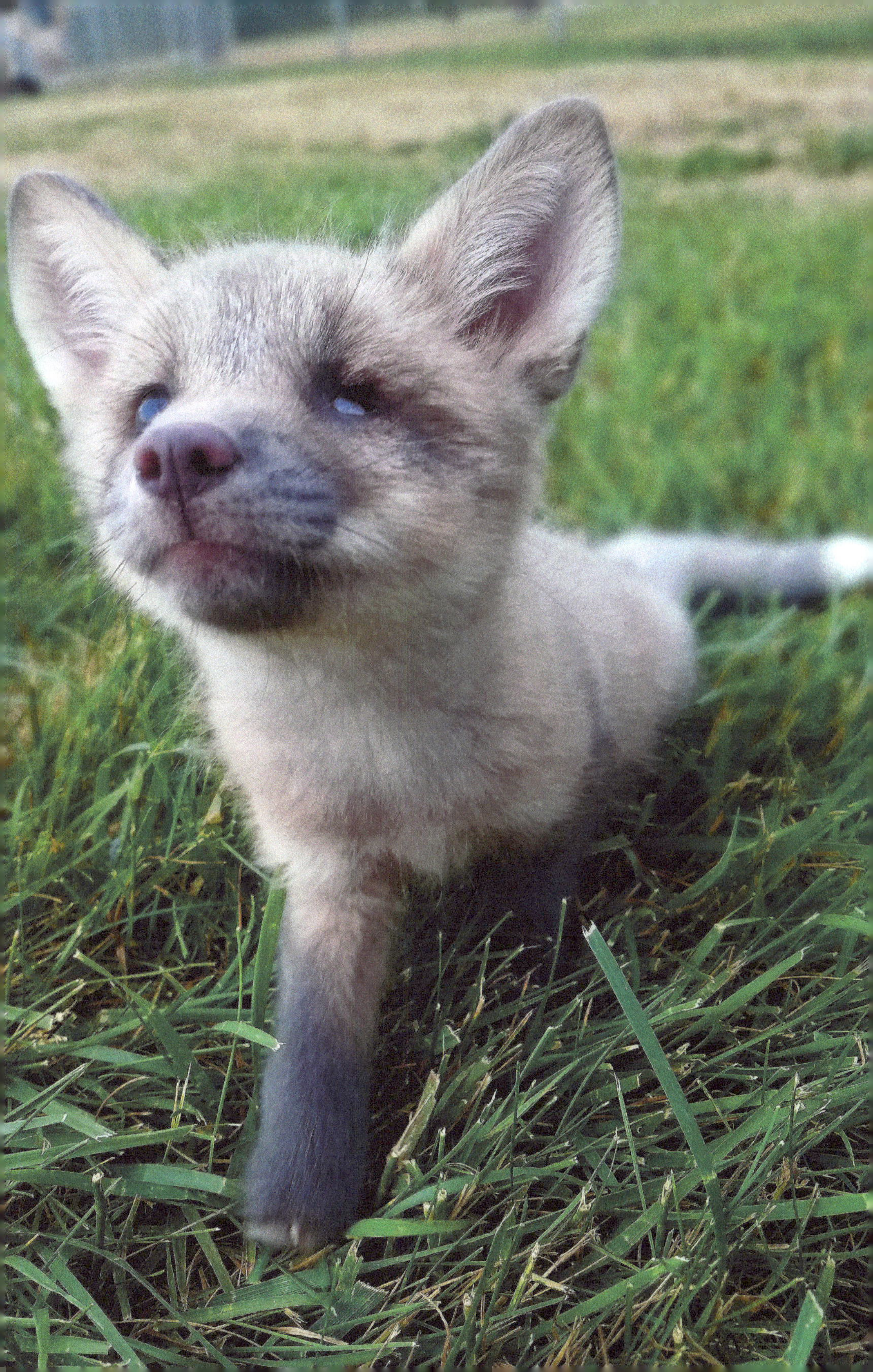

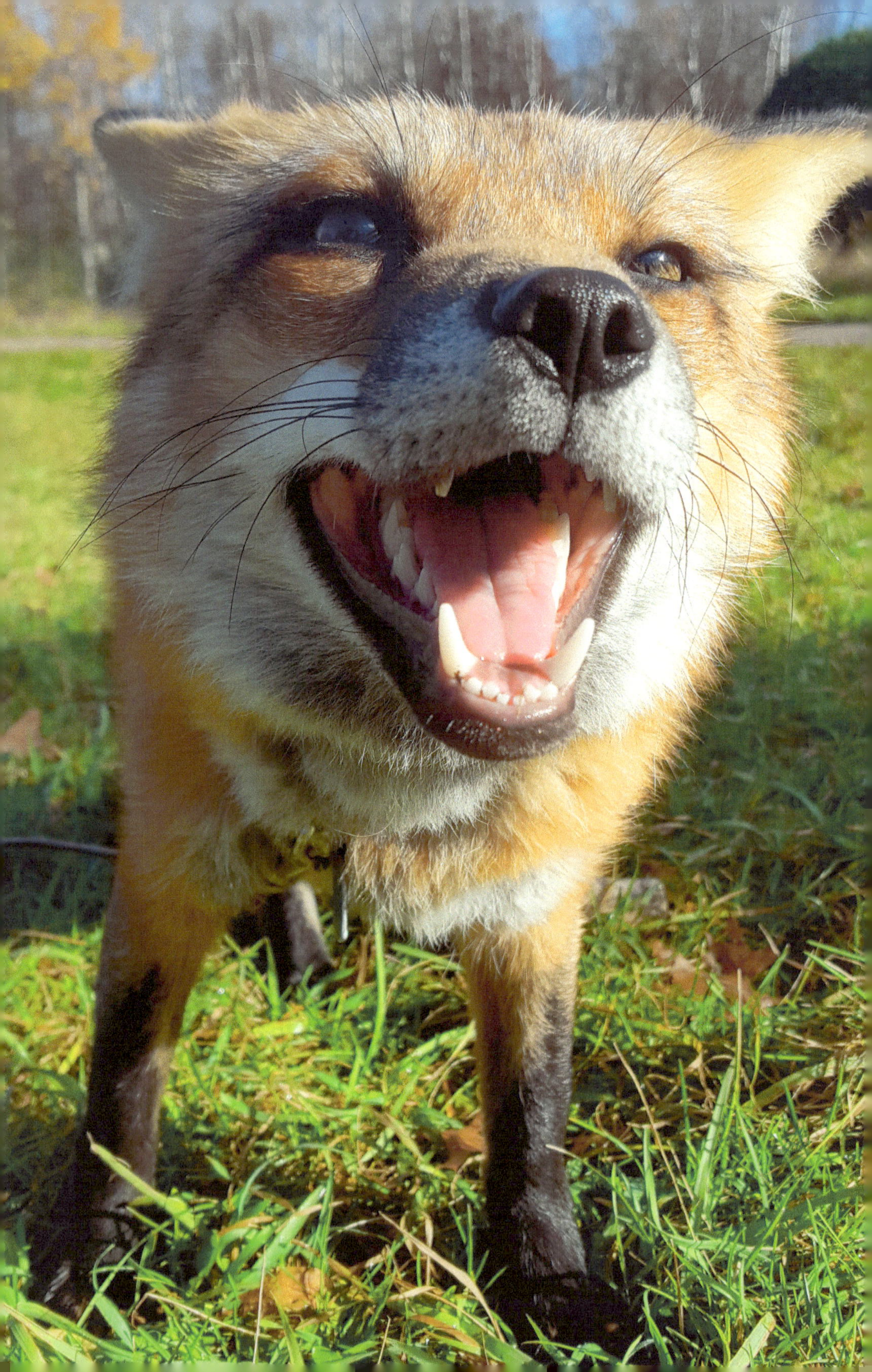

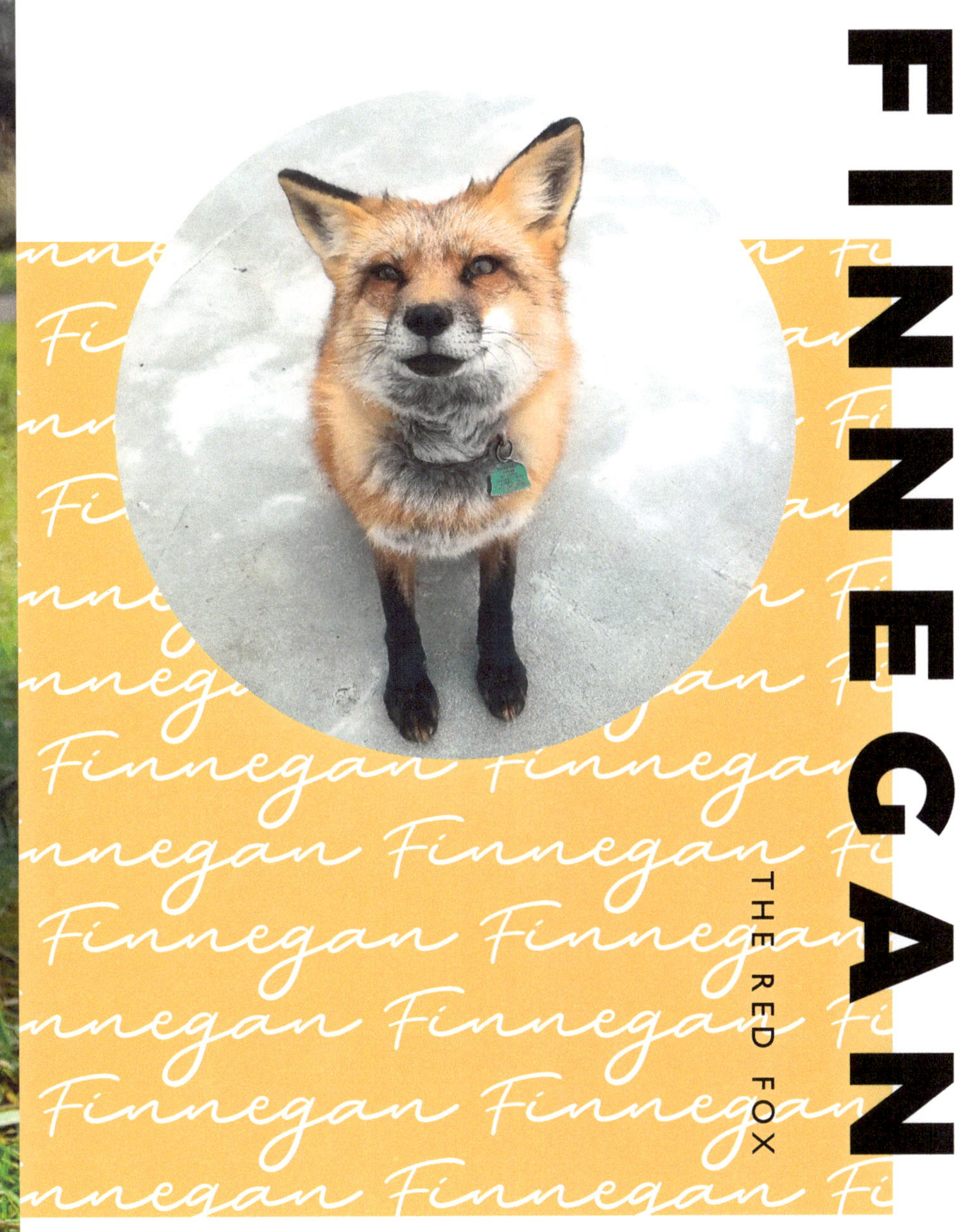

F I N N E G A N   was an extremely malnourished eight-month-old kit when he was surrendered to Mikayla in 2015. He was one of her first fox rescues, and she adopted him as her personal pet, making him a permanent resident of Save a Fox. Now, Finnegan is a happy, healthy fox, and one of the most sociable foxes on tours. Finn's best friend and mate is Dixie *(page 30)*, Mikayla's other pet fox.

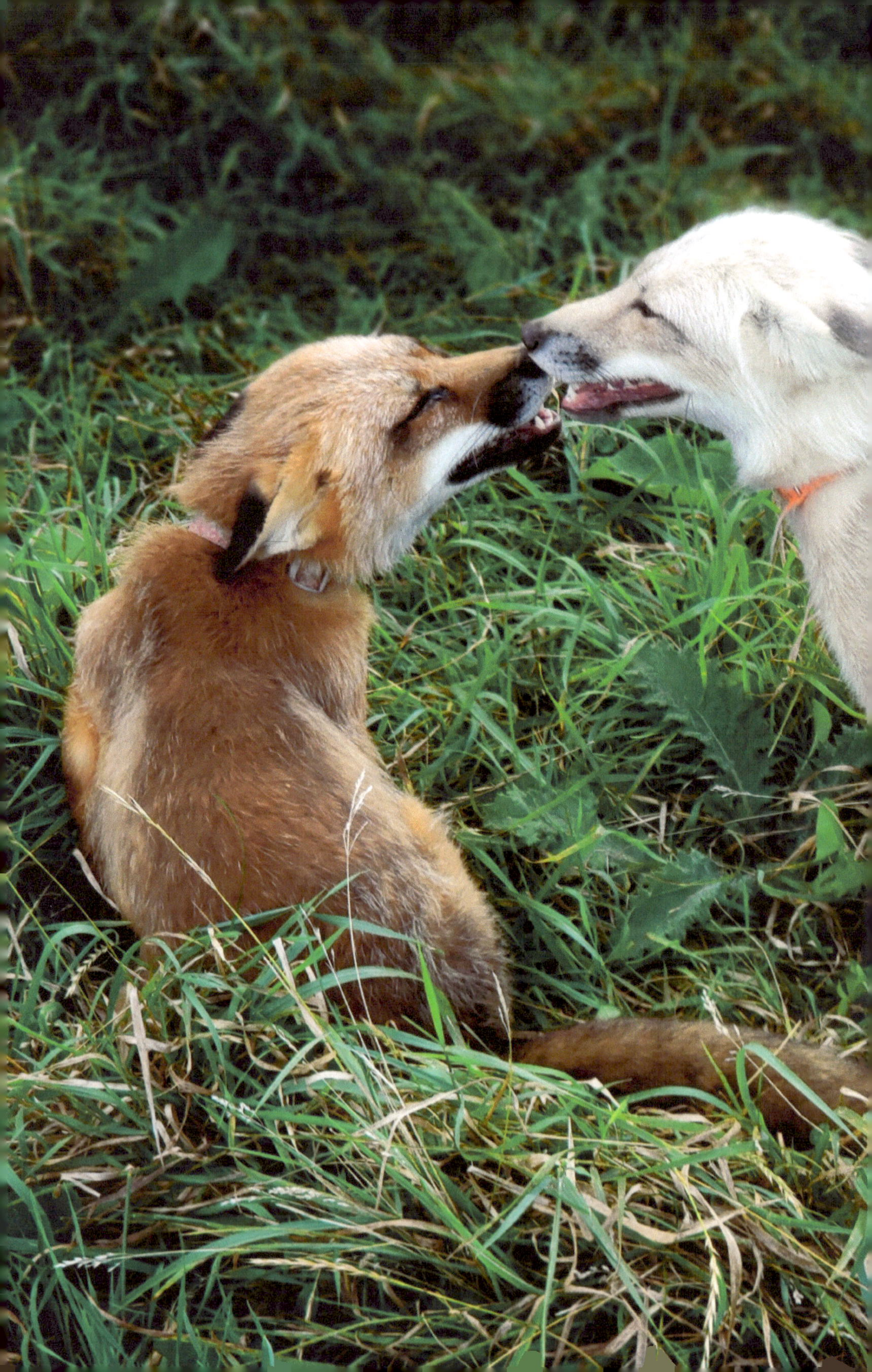

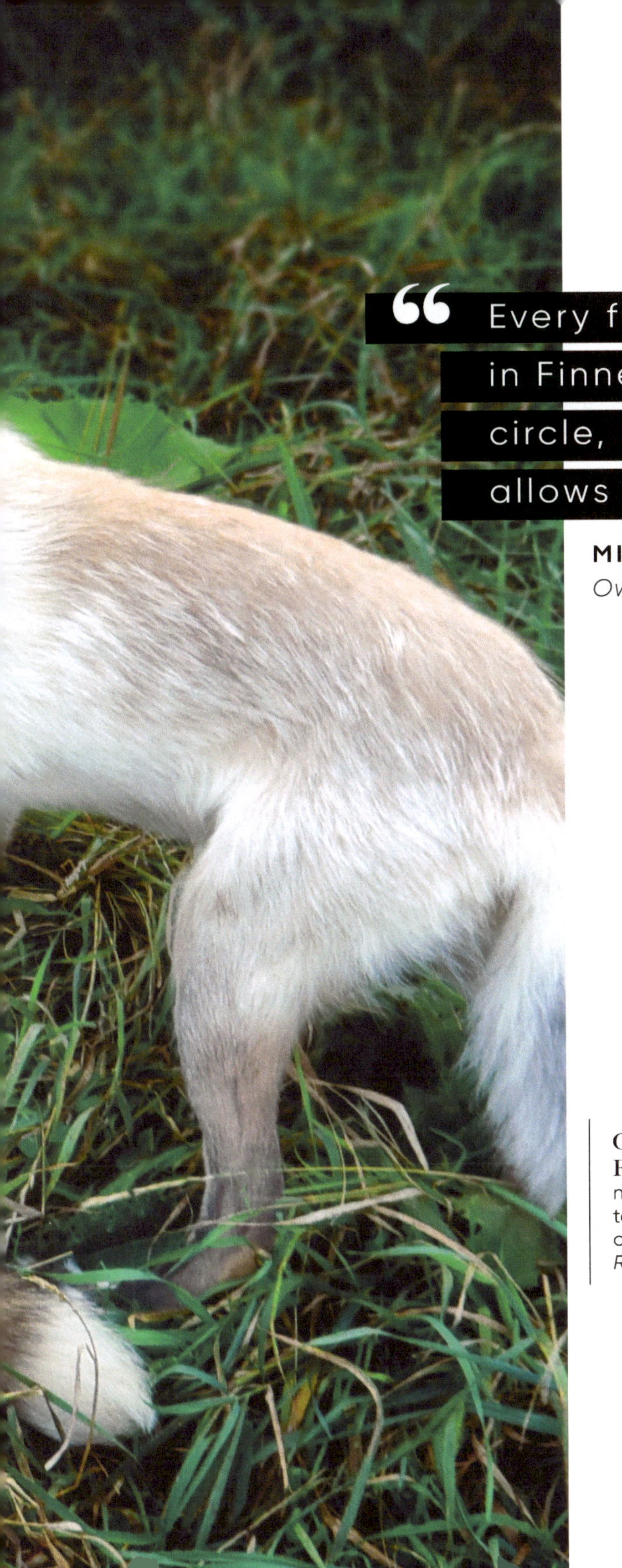

MIKAYLA RAINES
Owner of Save a Fox

OAKLEY AND FINNEGAN "boop" noses in the fox yard. Male foxes tend to get along with each other better than female foxes. *Read about Oakley on page 80.*

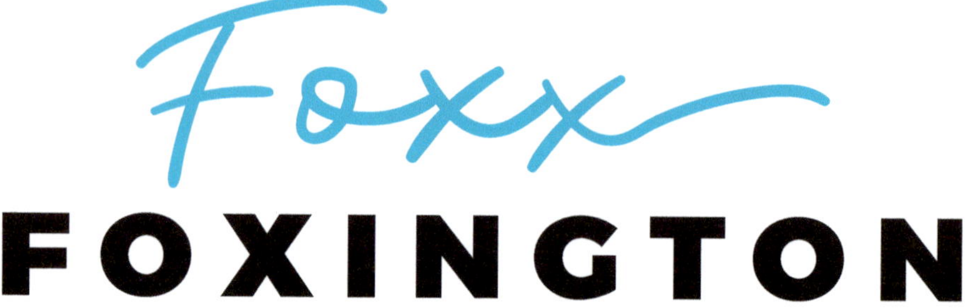

FOXINGTON

THE ARCTIC BLUE FOX

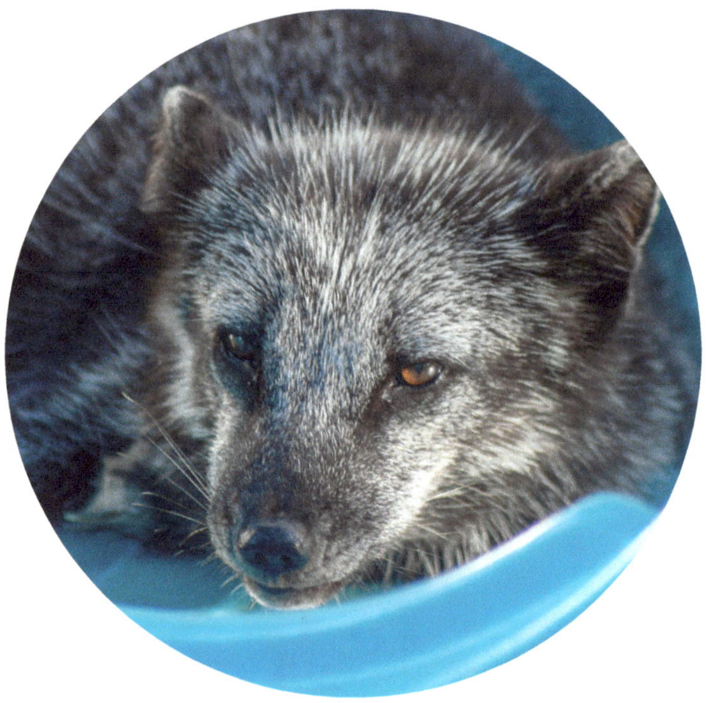

THE ARCTIC FOX is native to the frigid Arctic regions of the Northern Hemisphere, including Canada, Alaska, northern Asia, and northern Europe. With its thick coat, furry paw pads, and compact body, the arctic fox is well-adapted to living in sub-zero temperatures. In the winter, the arctic fox grows a thick, insulating white coat that blends into the snowy landscape. When the months grow warmer, it sheds down to a grayish-black or brown coat that camouflages with the darker summer environment. Foxington is a blue arctic fox, which means that his coat turns light gray or "blue" in the winter rather than bright white.

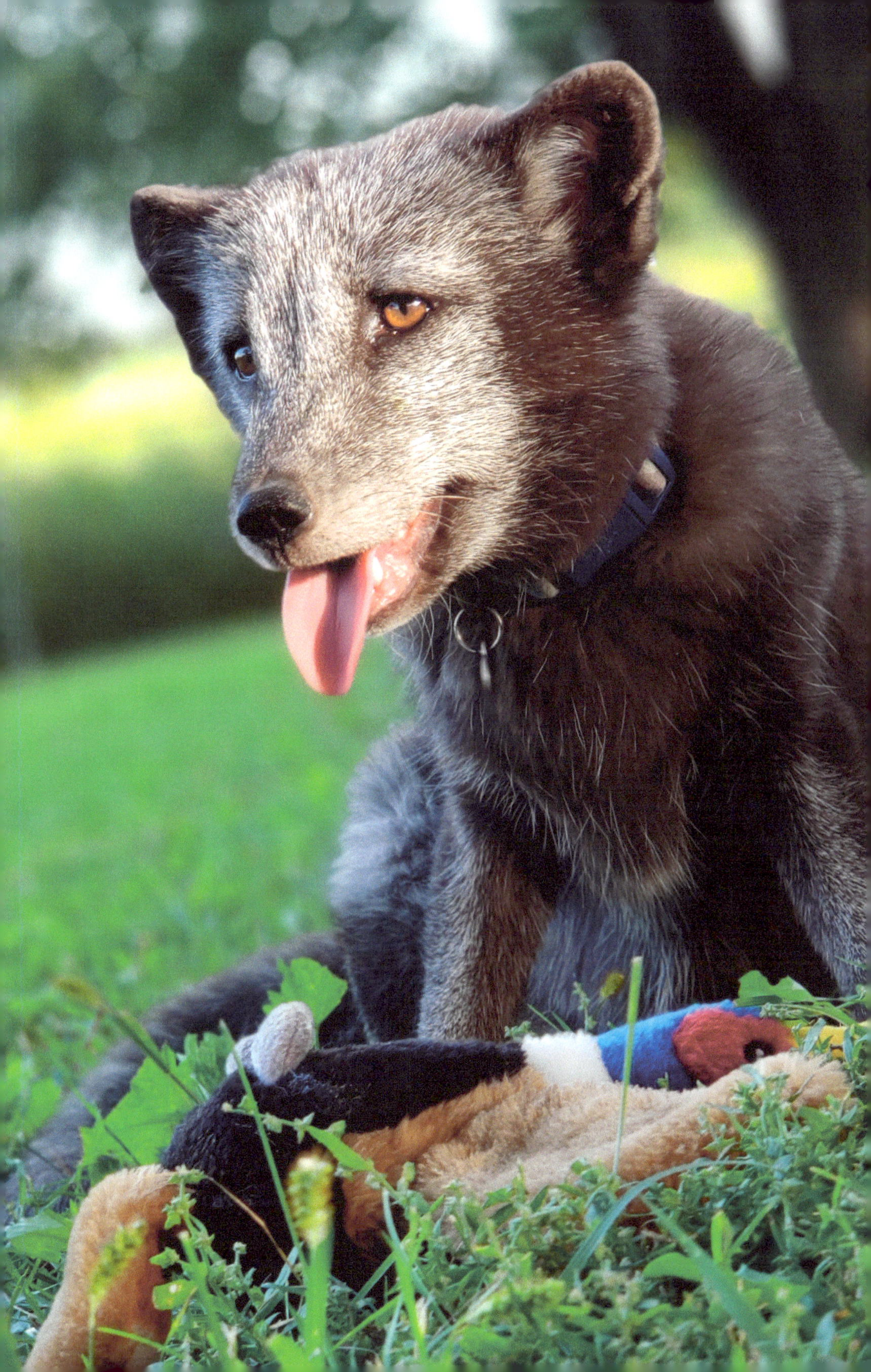

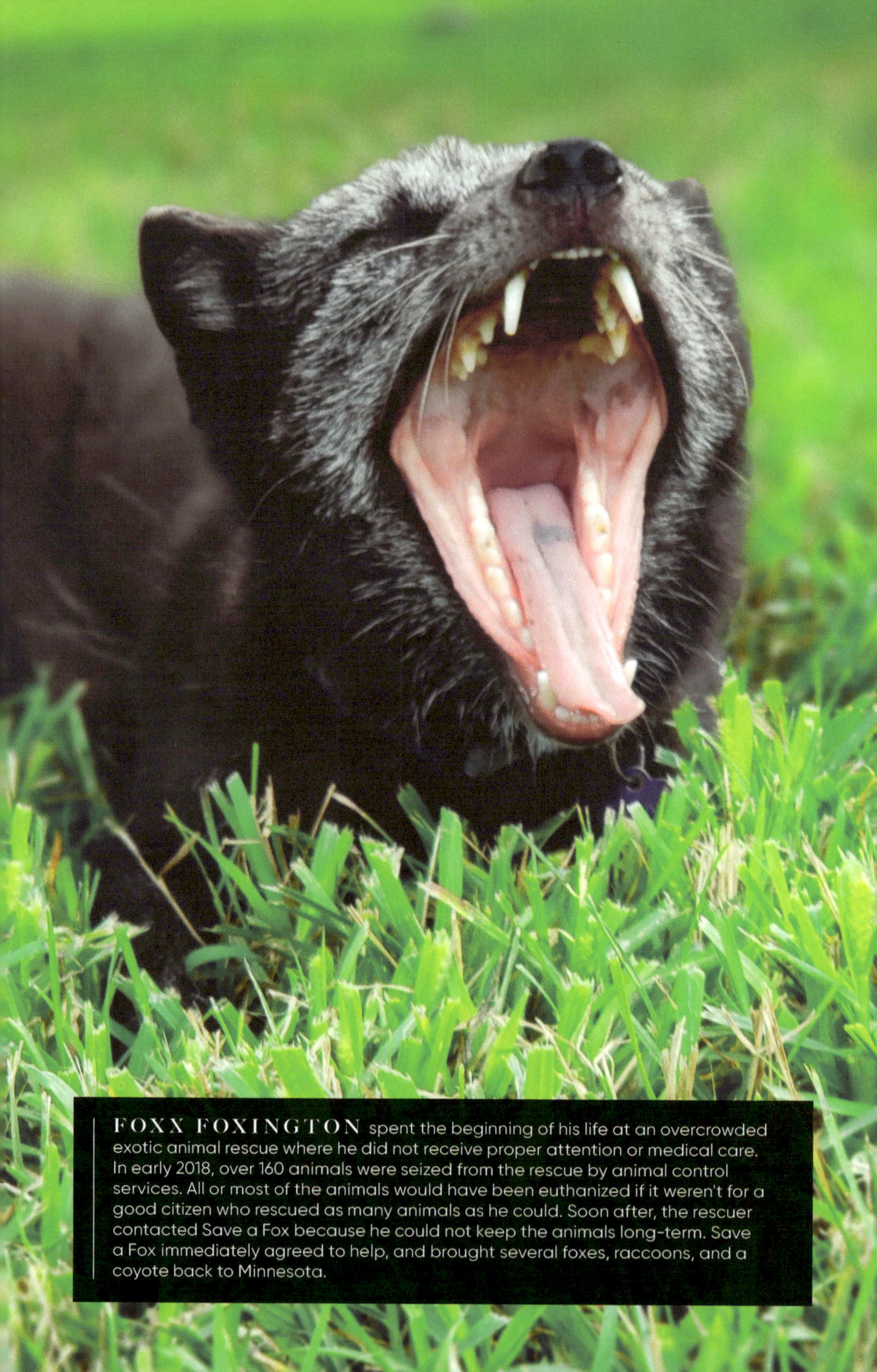

FOXX FOXINGTON spent the beginning of his life at an overcrowded exotic animal rescue where he did not receive proper attention or medical care. In early 2018, over 160 animals were seized from the rescue by animal control services. All or most of the animals would have been euthanized if it weren't for a good citizen who rescued as many animals as he could. Soon after, the rescuer contacted Save a Fox because he could not keep the animals long-term. Save a Fox immediately agreed to help, and brought several foxes, raccoons, and a coyote back to Minnesota.

> **In the spring, Foxx Foxington molts his winter coat just like the red foxes, but his appearance changes entirely—from a big fluffy white marshmallow in the winter, to a silver-tipped black in the summer.**
>
> **MIKAYLA RAINES**
> *Owner of Save a Fox*

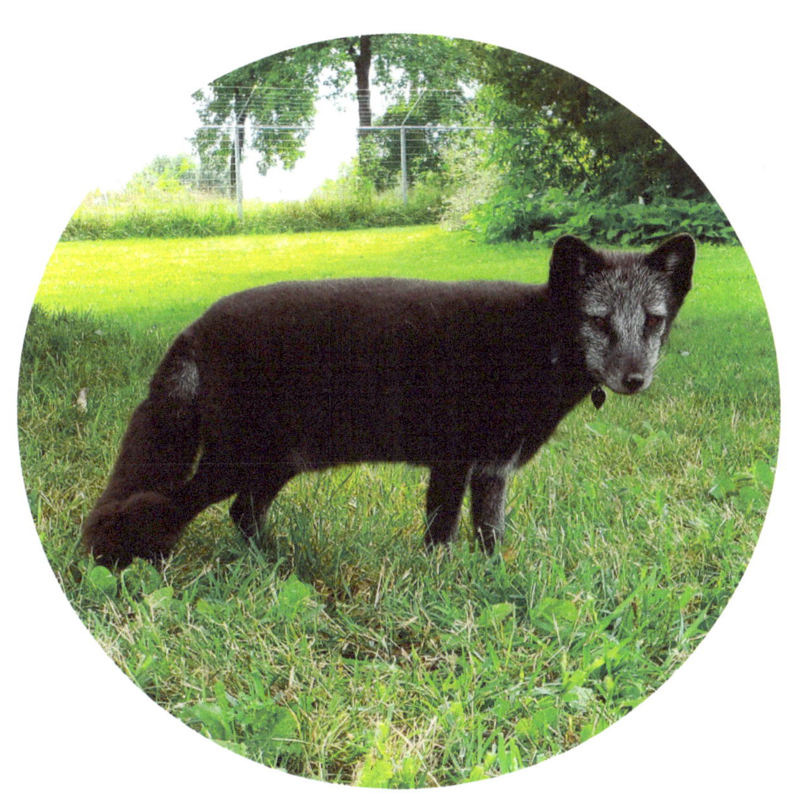

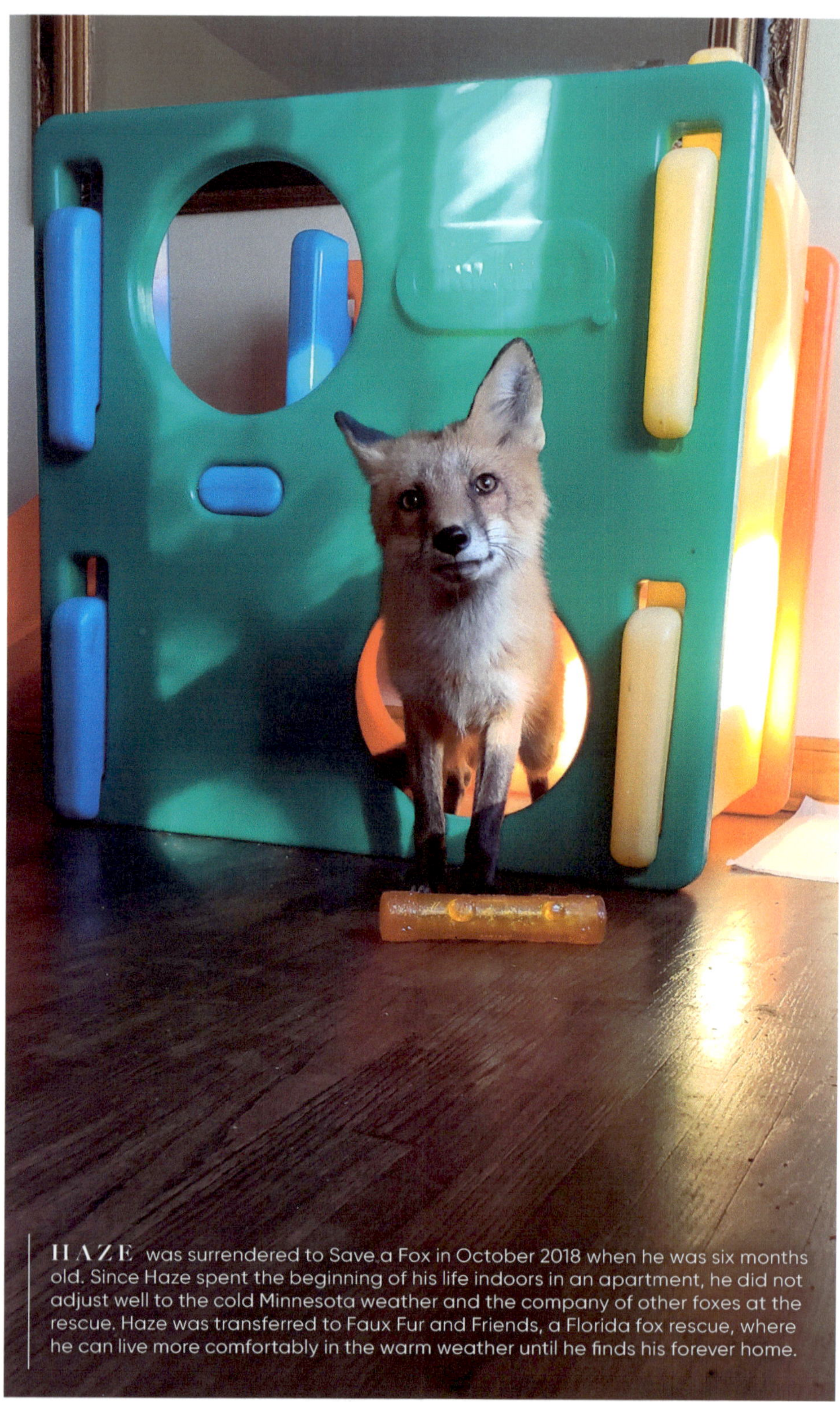

HAZE was surrendered to Save a Fox in October 2018 when he was six months old. Since Haze spent the beginning of his life indoors in an apartment, he did not adjust well to the cold Minnesota weather and the company of other foxes at the rescue. Haze was transferred to Faux Fur and Friends, a Florida fox rescue, where he can live more comfortably in the warm weather until he finds his forever home.

HAZE

THE RED FOX

"

The first couple days are always very scary. [The foxes] don't understand where they are, why they are here, or when they will 'go home.' I wish I could just tell Haze everything is going to be all right, but he doesn't understand. I can't wait to see him come out of his shell and show his personality.

MIKAYLA RAINES
Owner of Save a Fox

"

JOKER

THE MARBLE FOX

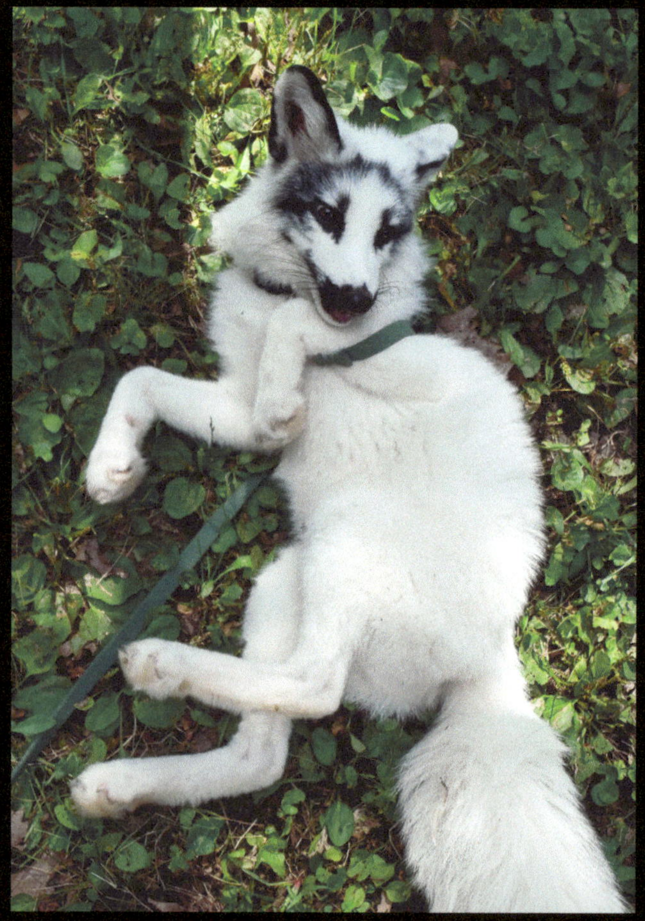

JOKER was obtained by animal control services in August 2018 after he was found running loose in the city of Rochester, Minnesota—a city where pet foxes are not allowed. When no owner came to claim him, animal control contacted Save a Fox. The rescue took Joker in, and he was adopted just a few months later. Joker now lives with a fellow Save a Fox rescue, Milo.

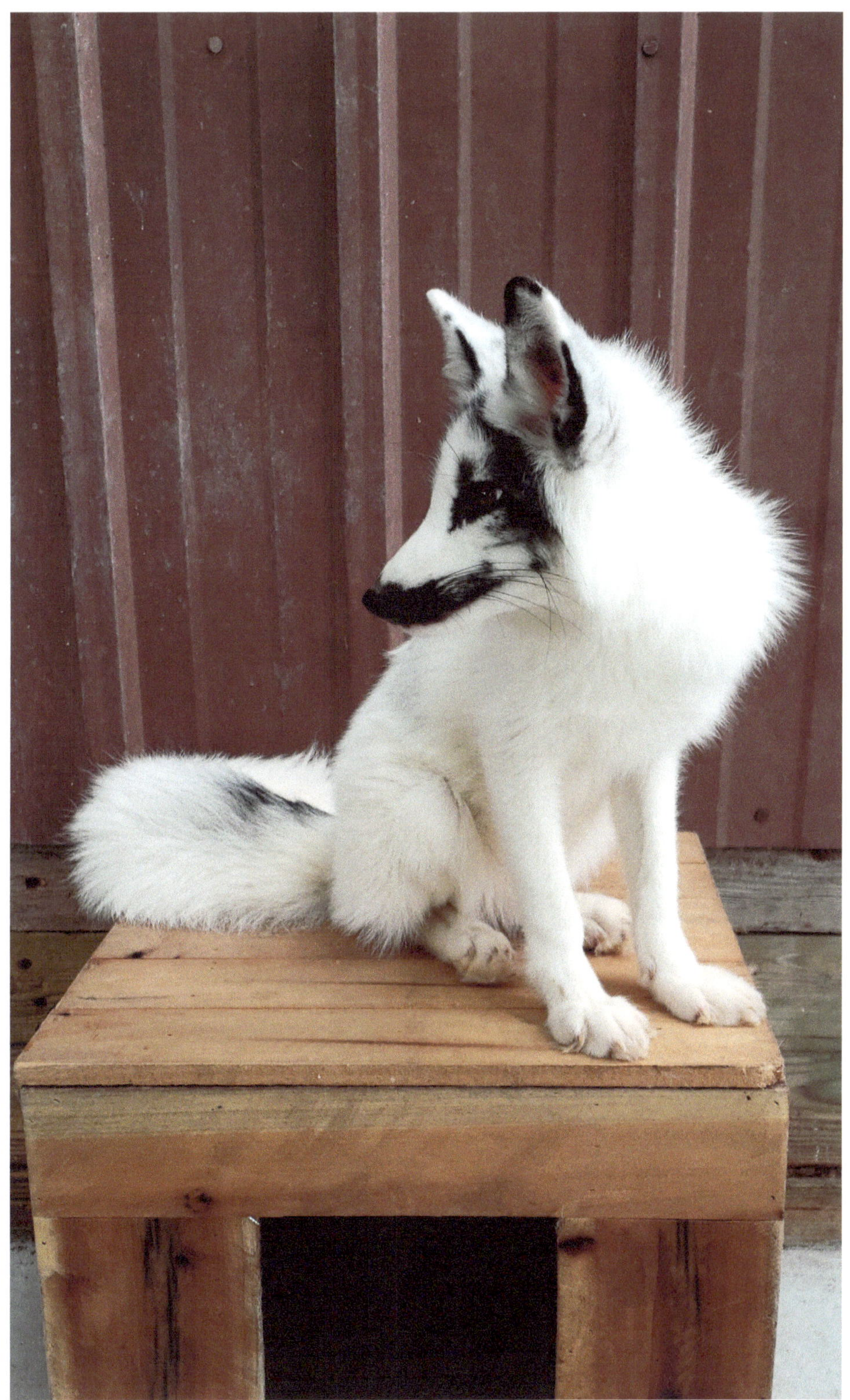

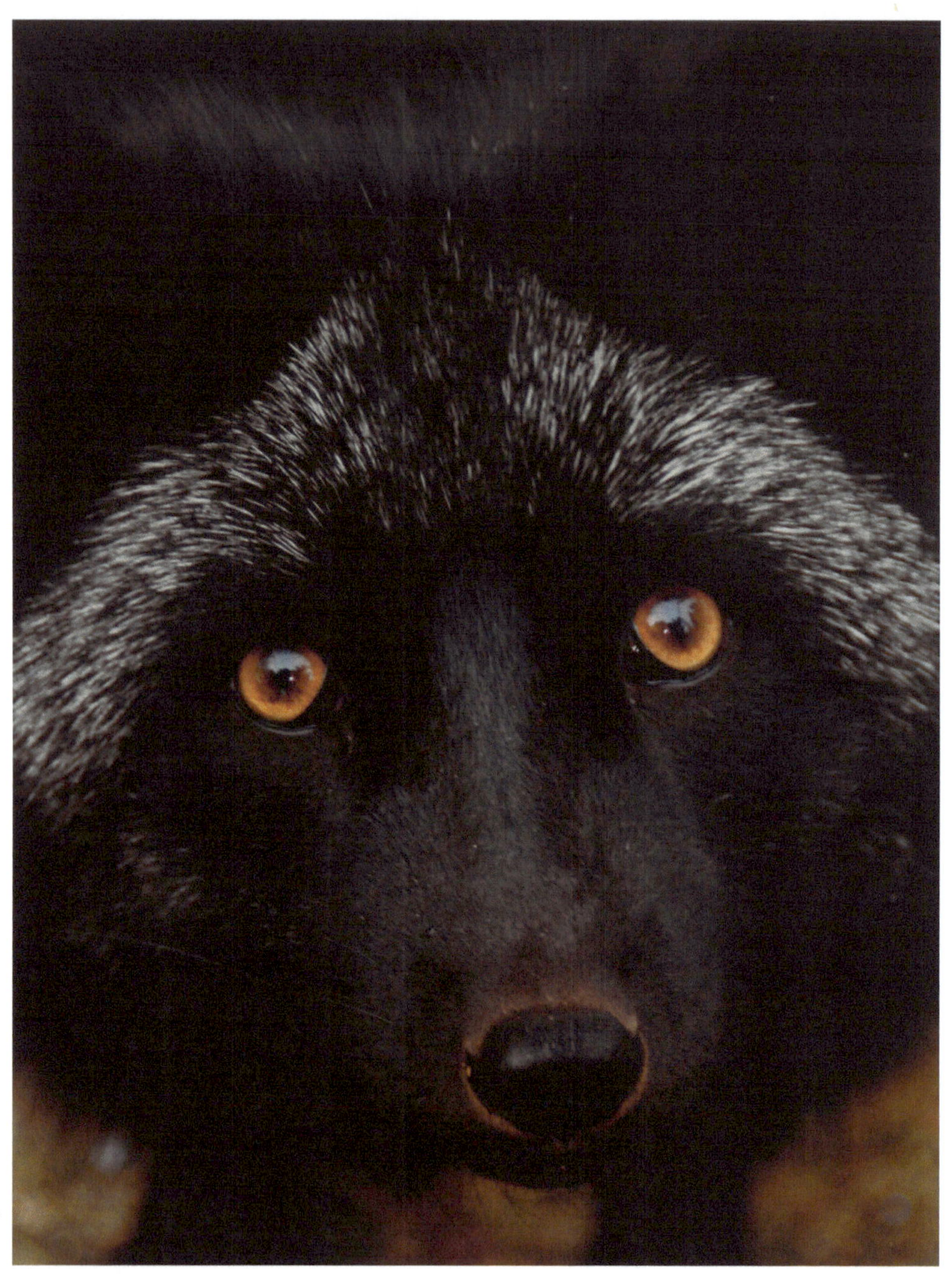

Liska is shy, but very sweet.
I can tell she is a lover.

MIKAYLA RAINES
Owner of Save a Fox

LISKA

THE SILVER FOX

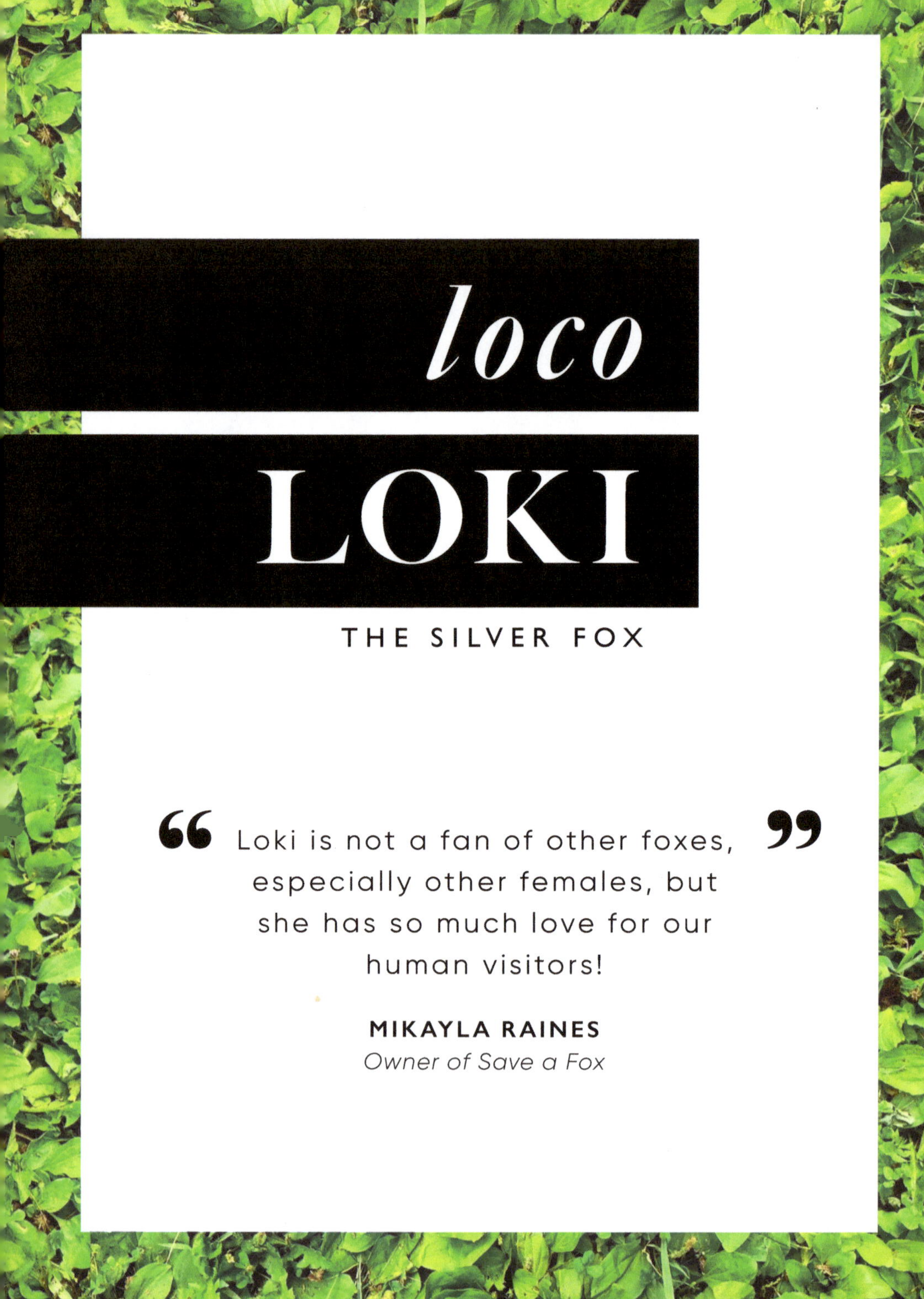
loco
LOKI
THE SILVER FOX

"
Loki is not a fan of other foxes,
especially other females, but
she has so much love for our
human visitors!
"
MIKAYLA RAINES
Owner of Save a Fox

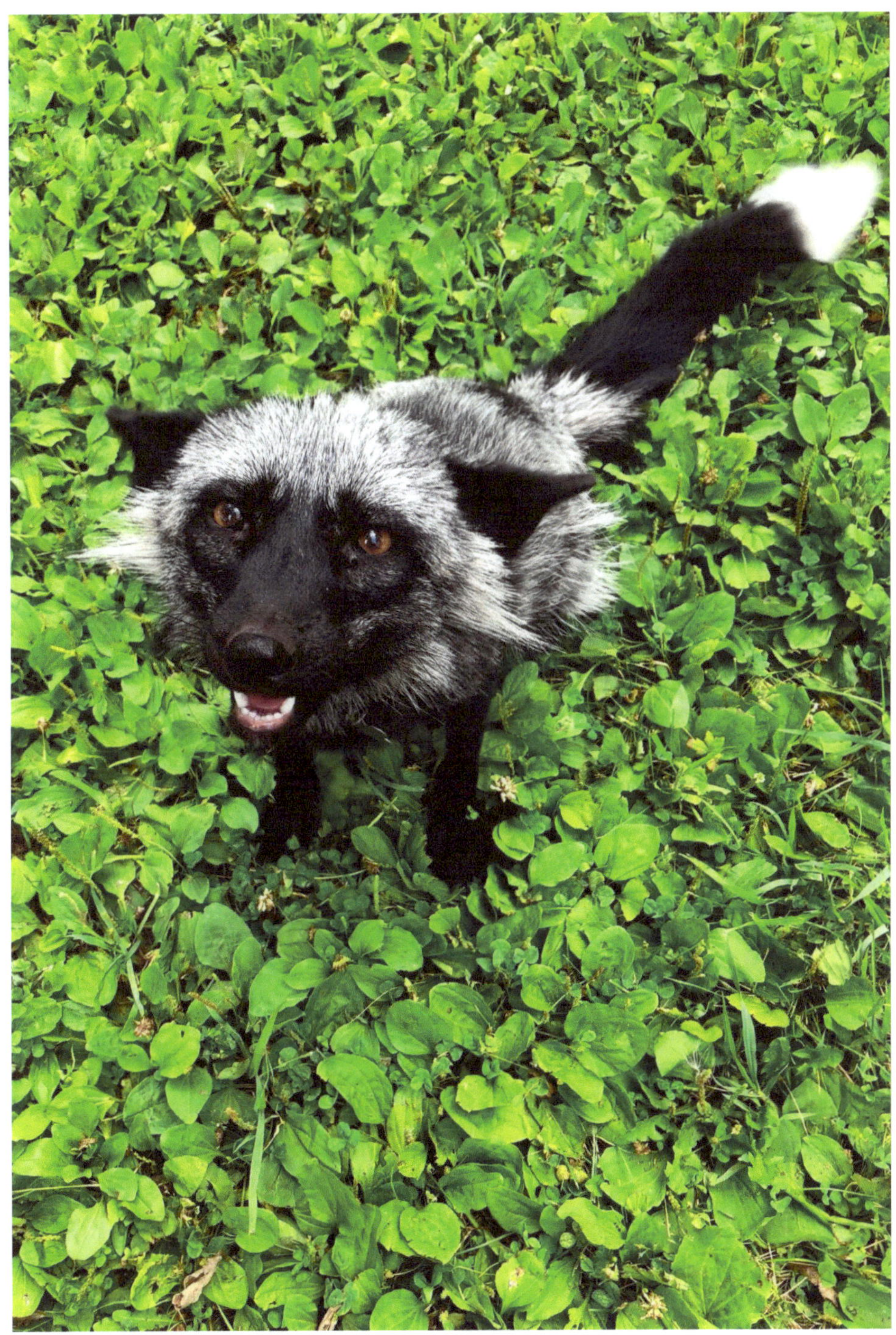

LOKI was a pet fox who was surrendered to Save a Fox in August 2017. She was adopted by a loving family, and is now called Smokey.

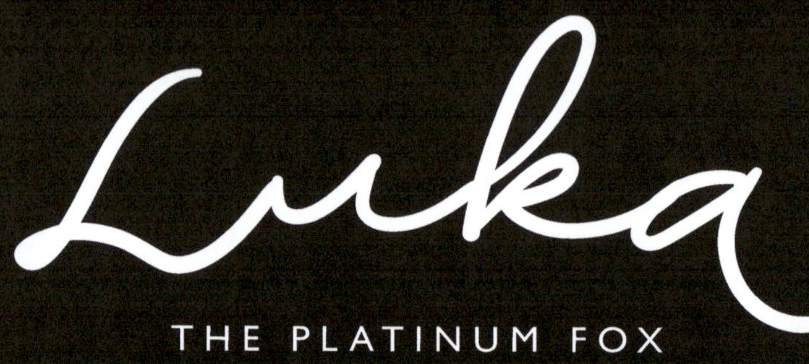

THE PLATINUM FOX

> "
>
> Of the Furfarm trio—Luka, Jack, and Scarlett—Luka is having the most trouble making friends. His body language is a little forward, and the other foxes are taking it as a challenge! He may or may not get better in time. We will continue introducing him to one new fox at a time [...] Like kids at a playground, not all foxes get along. Which is why we have five separate fox yards, and we only let the foxes out in specific groups within each yard.
>
> **MIKAYLA RAINES**
> *Owner of Save a Fox*
>
> "

LUKA was rescued from a fur farm in June 2018 along with two other foxes named Scarlett (*page 8*) and Captain Jack (*page 28*). The three are known as "The Trio" around the rescue. Luka has a fatherly instinct with kits, and loves playing with them.

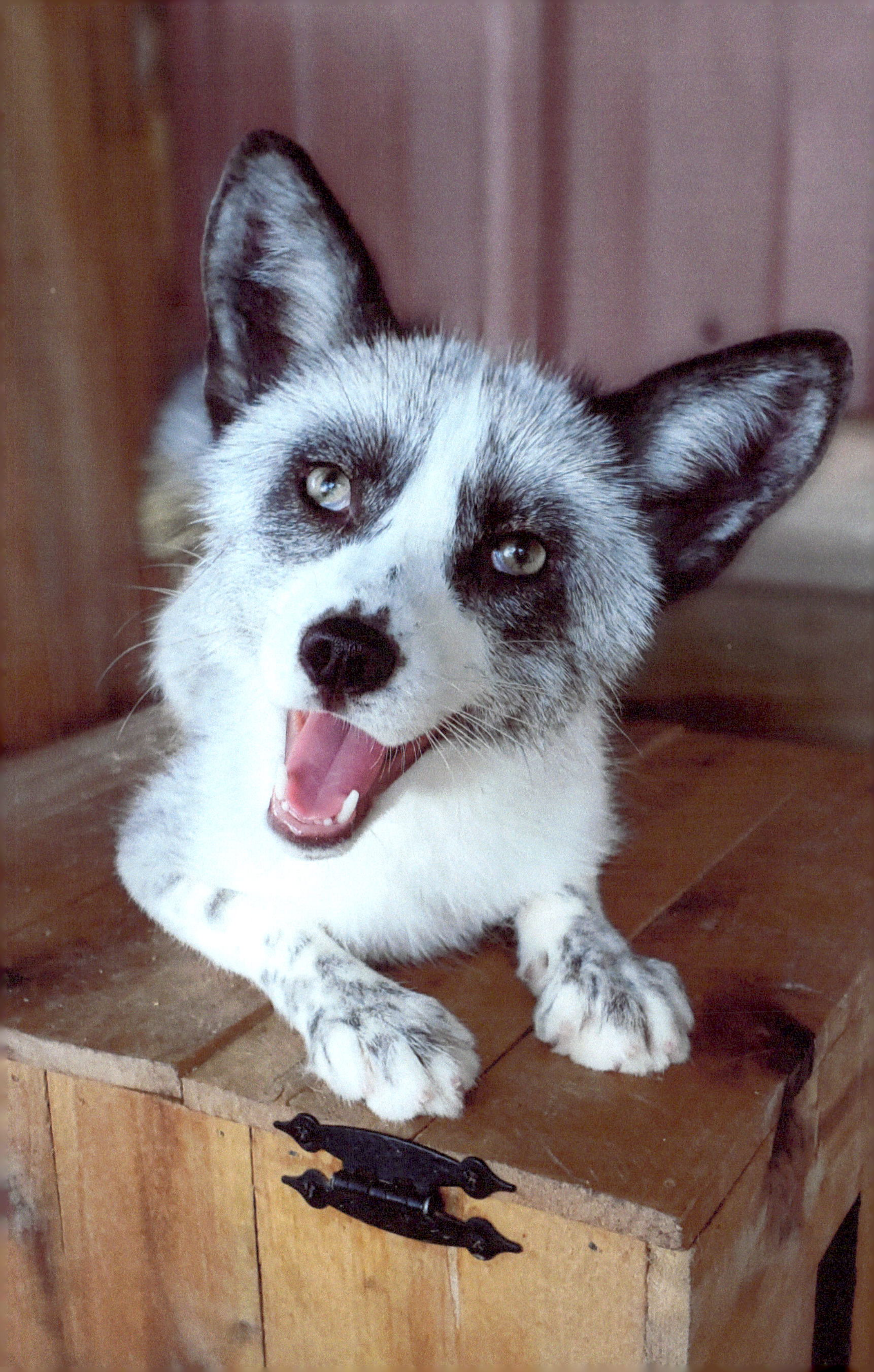

Lumi

THE BLUE ARCTIC FOX

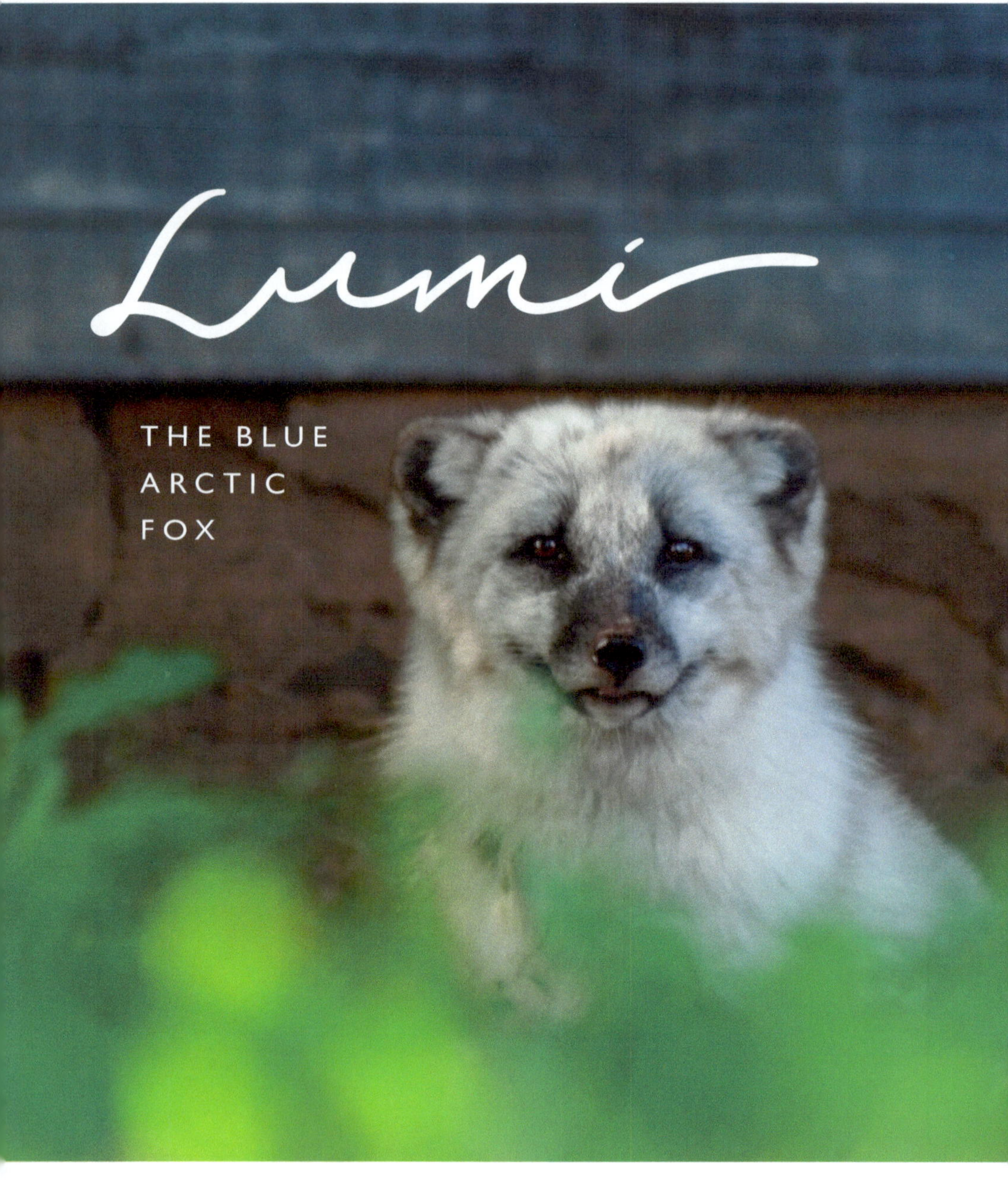

LUMI is one of the shyest foxes at the rescue. She rarely takes treats from volunteers, and prefers to hide away during photoshoots. Lumi shares a fox yard with Foxx Foxington *(page 56)*, the only other arctic fox currently at the rescue.

ABOVE RIGHT: Lumi's internal clock was incorrect as a result of living indoors for most of her life, and she began molting in mid-September of 2019 when her coat should have been thickening in preparation for the cool autumn season.

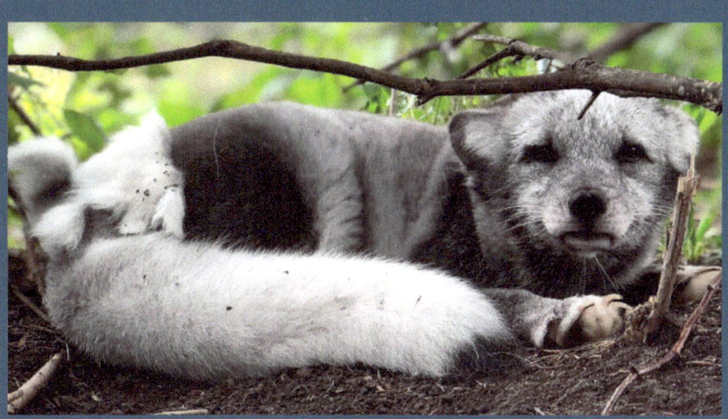

MIKAYLA RAINES
Owner of Save a Fox

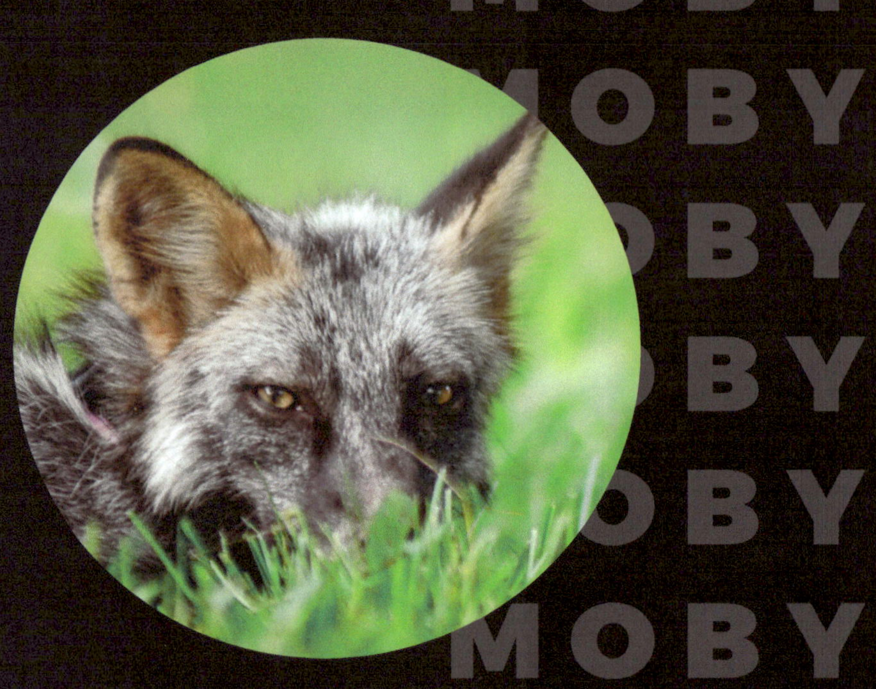

MOBY

THE MOON GLOW FOX

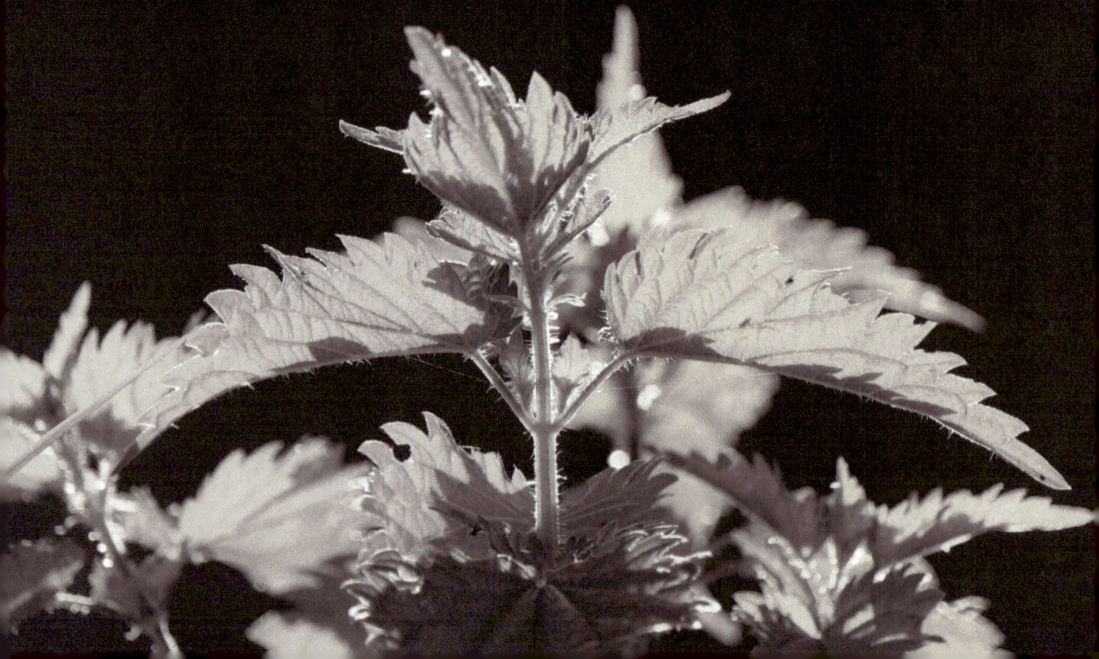

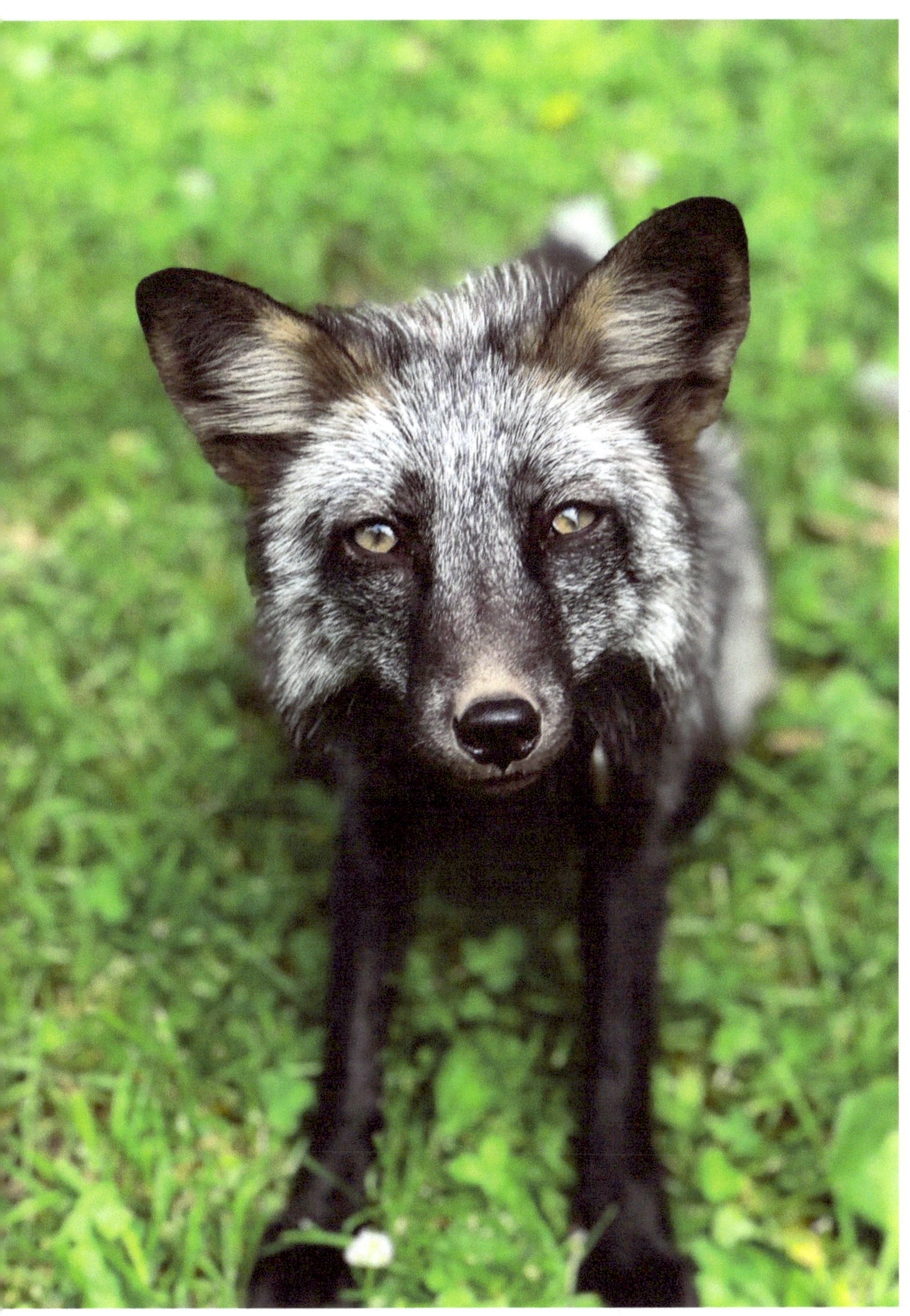

THE MOON GLOW FOX coloration doesn't occur naturally in the wild. It is the result of selectively breeding several generations of red foxes crossed with silver foxes. Moon glow foxes have primarily gray or black bodies with light orange or beige markings on their faces and sides.

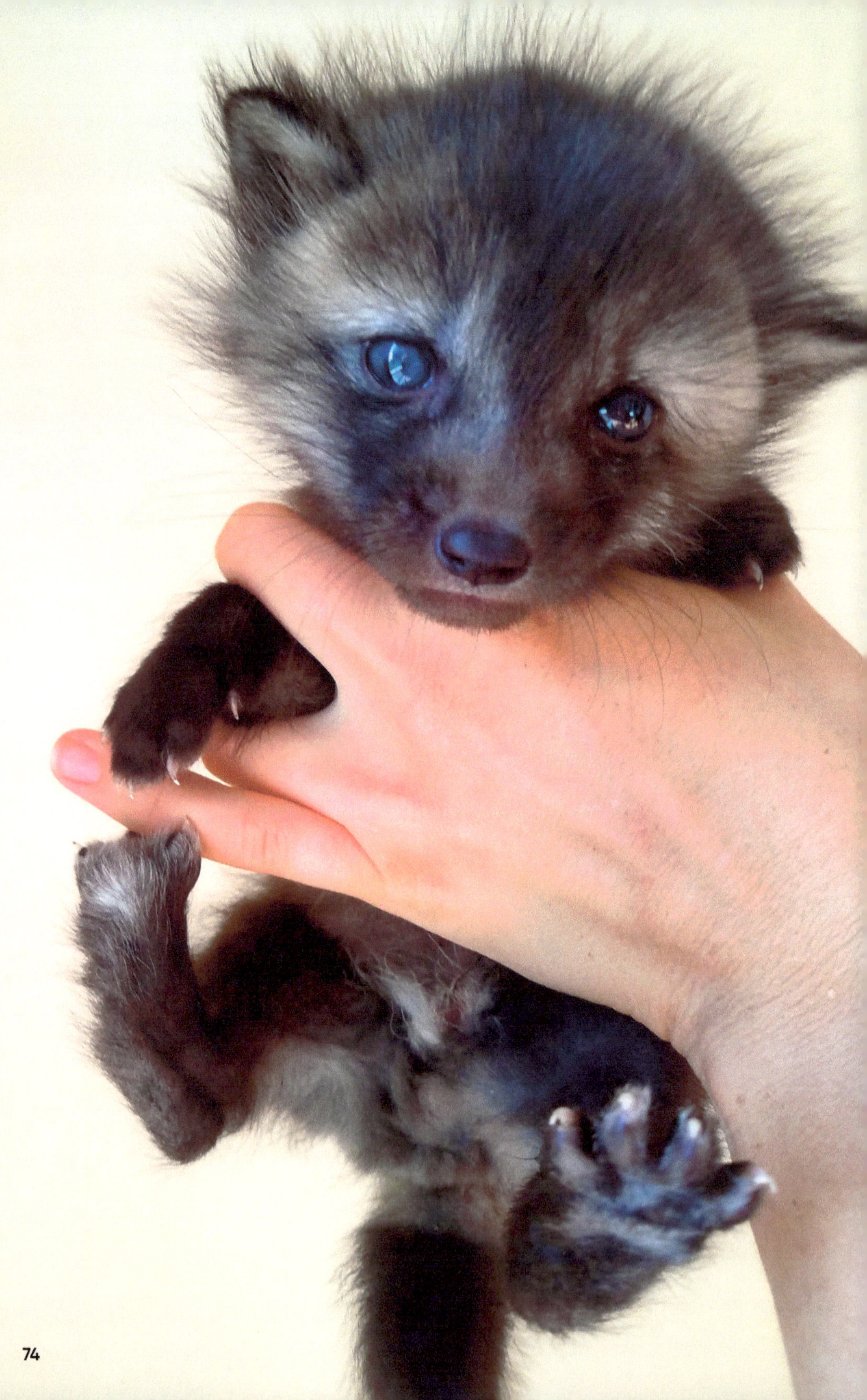

I've never cared for a fox quite like Moby. It's like living with a newborn who never stops crying. He cries when he is alone, cries when he has company, cries when he is held, cries when he has play time, cries while he is eating [...] He is not showing any signs of pain, and his injury is starting to heal up. He is still on antibiotics, pain meds, and wears his honey bandages at night. There is nothing we can do to make him stop crying. We are starting to realize this might just be how he is. He might just be special... He is very vocal, and definitely no normal fox pup.

MIKAYLA RAINES
Owner of Save a Fox

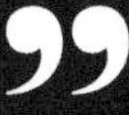

MOBY was rescued from a fur farm in June 2018. He came to the rescue with severe wounds from being carried too roughly by his mother. For several stressful weeks he received around-the-clock care, and it was unclear if he would survive. Happily, Moby made a full recovery, and has stopped crying so often.

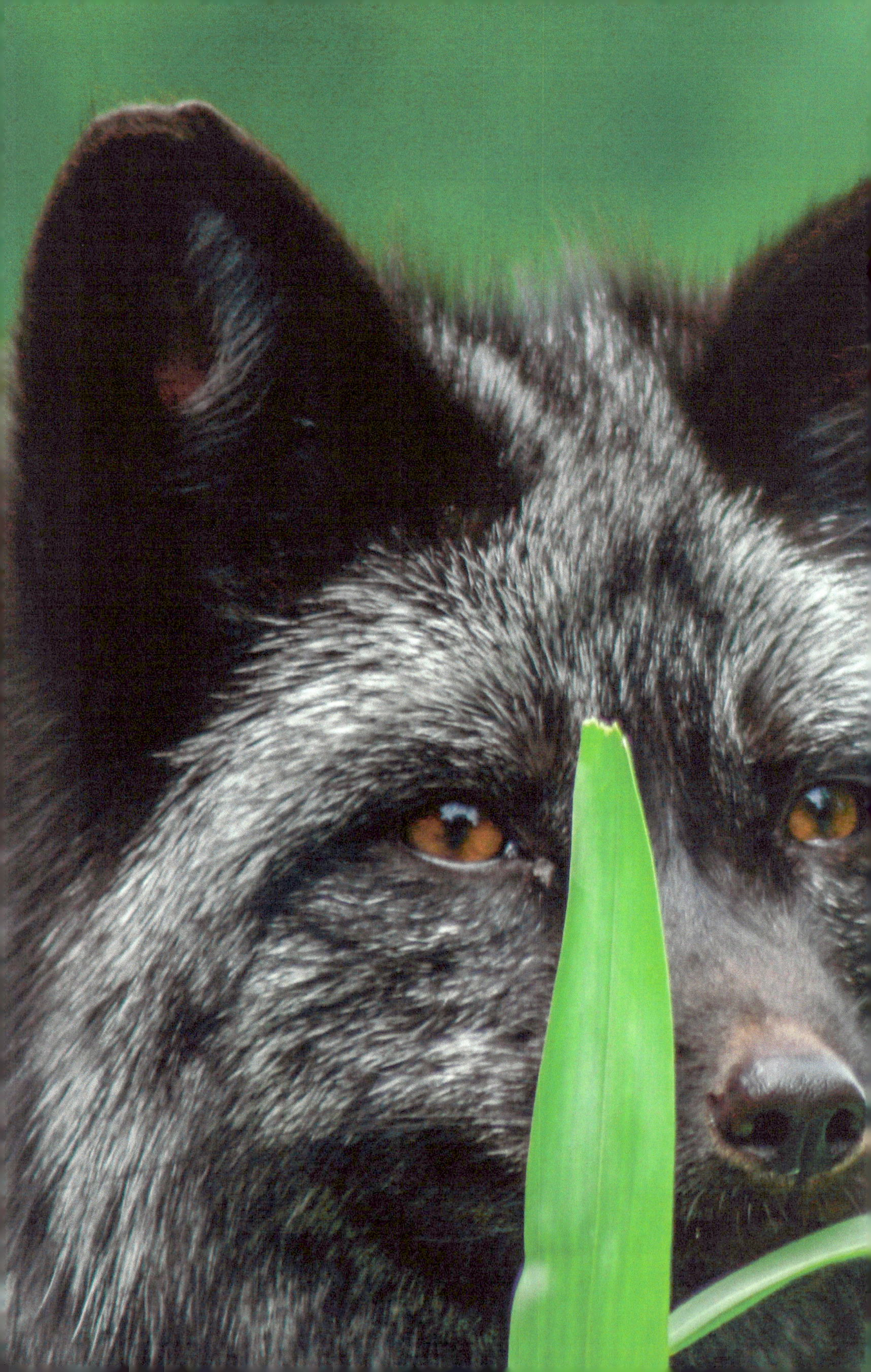

MUTTIAS

THE SILVER FOX

"

So far, Mutt has shown himself to be the best indoor pet surrender we've ever had. For a fox, he isn't very high maintenance. He's well mannered, and he will make a great indoor fox for the right person. I feel it is important to note that most foxes DO NOT make good indoor pets. Most foxes prefer to be outdoors—even Mutt gets plenty of outdoor time. Foxes can never be 100% potty trained. Mutt uses his litterbox 60% of the time, which is considered REALLY good for a fox.

MIKAYLA RAINES
Owner of Save a Fox

"

MUTTIAS, a.k.a. "Mutt," went through two families before he was one year old. His first familiy wasn't able to properly care for him, and passed him on to his second owner, who lived in an apartment. His second owner soon realized that she could not keep Muttias in an apartment, and contacted Save a Fox, who immediately agreed to take him in. "We do not adopt out to apartment buildings, considering those are where most of our pet surrenders come from," Mikayla said. "Foxes and apartments do not work." Around the rescue, Mutt is best friends with Vixie the silver fox *(page 98)* and Batty Artemis the gray fox *(page 20)*.

Nikita

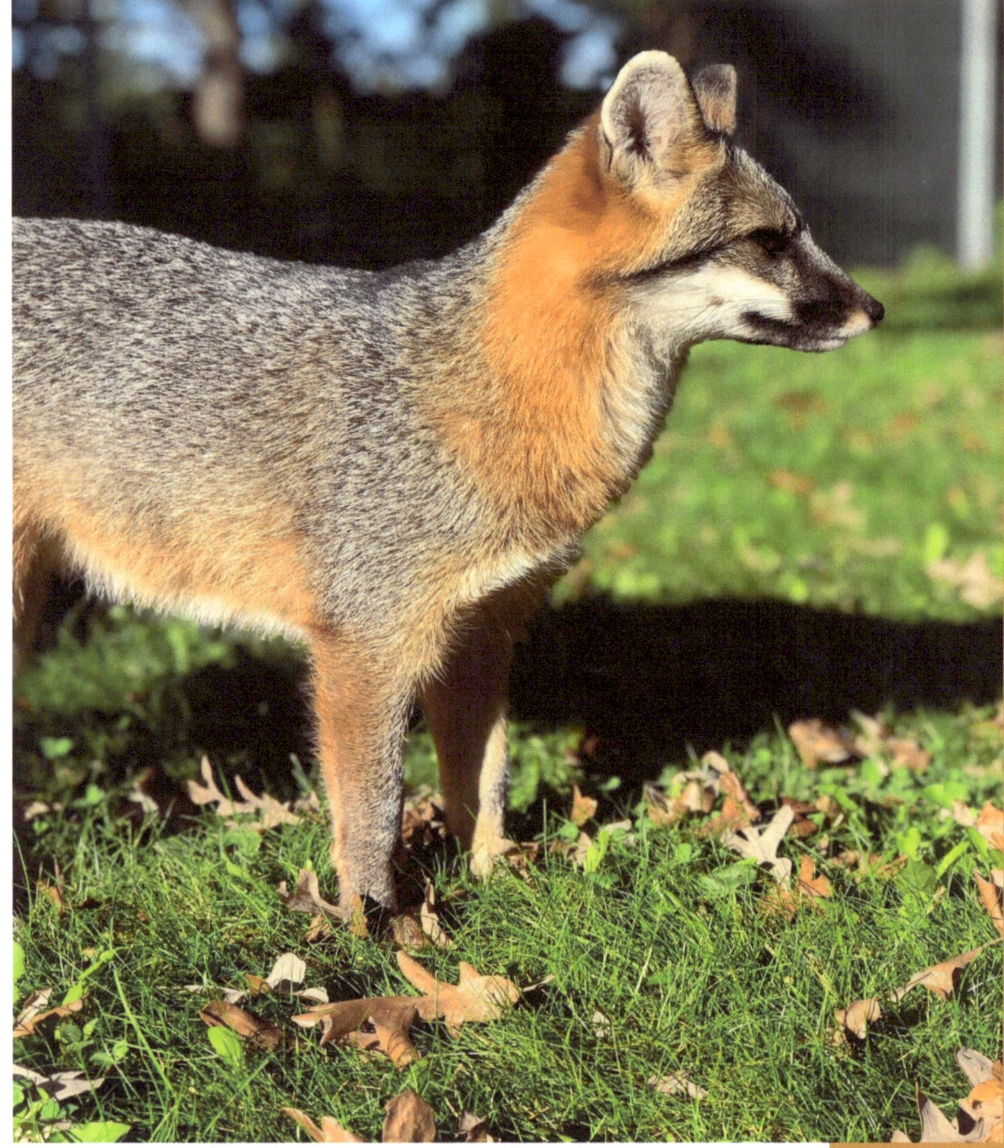

N I K I T A is the first female gray fox at the rescue. She enjoys sun basking outside in the heat of the day—even though gray foxes are nocturnal.

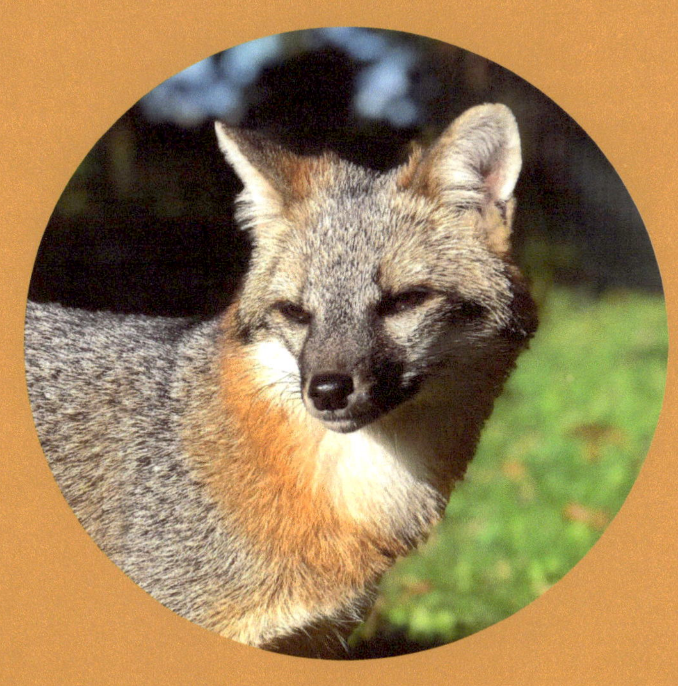

> Nikita came from a breeder. She was the only unchosen kit in her litter. At six months old and completely wild, no one wanted her. I took her in. The first week with her was hell. She lunged at me and bit me. I never thought she would come around. But eventually, we were sharing snacks in bed.

MIKAYLA RAINES
Owner of Save a Fox

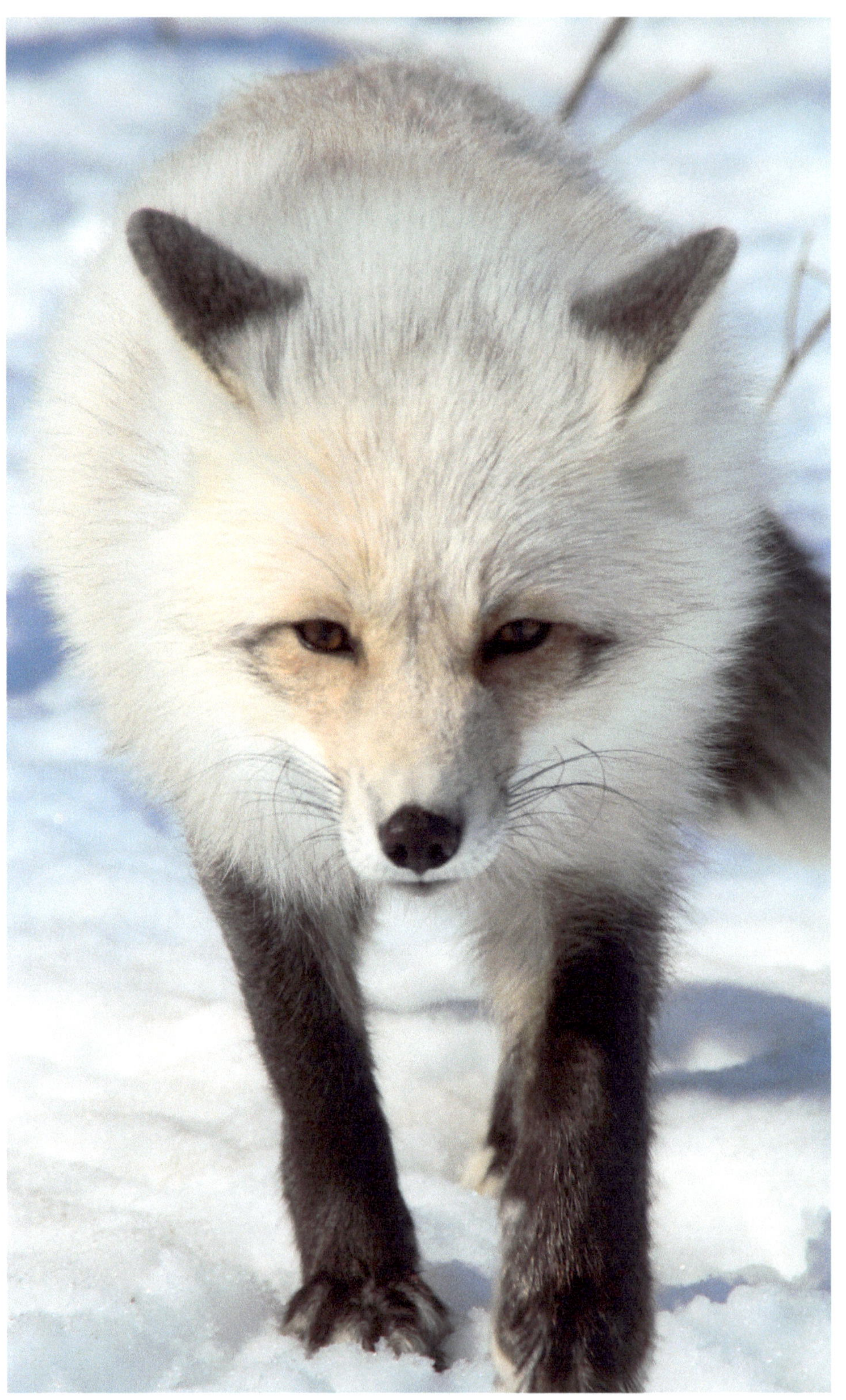

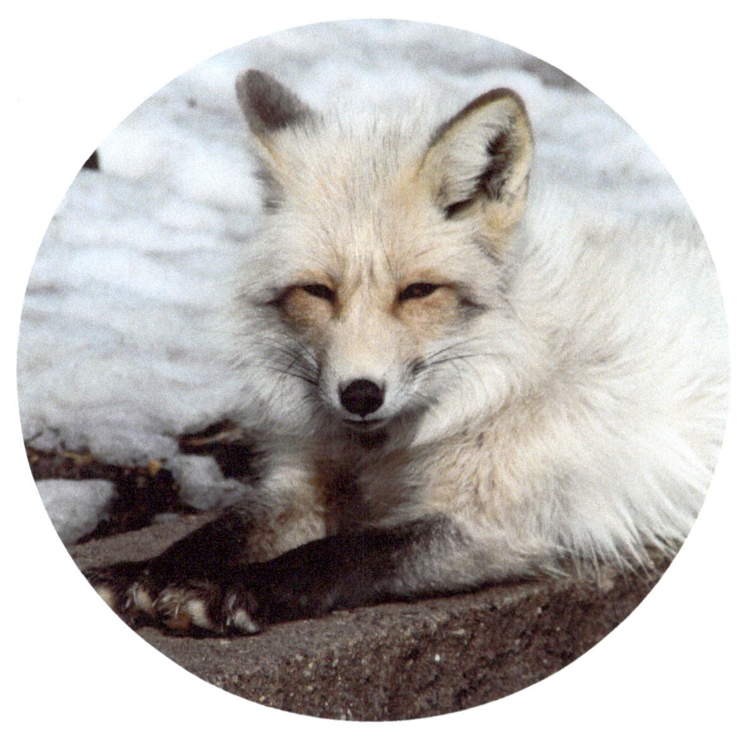

OAKLEY

THE FIRE AND ICE FOX

THE FIRE AND ICE FOX is a color variation of the red fox that was developed in the fur farming industry. It is lighter and more cream colored than a regular red fox with light gray or blueish "stockings."

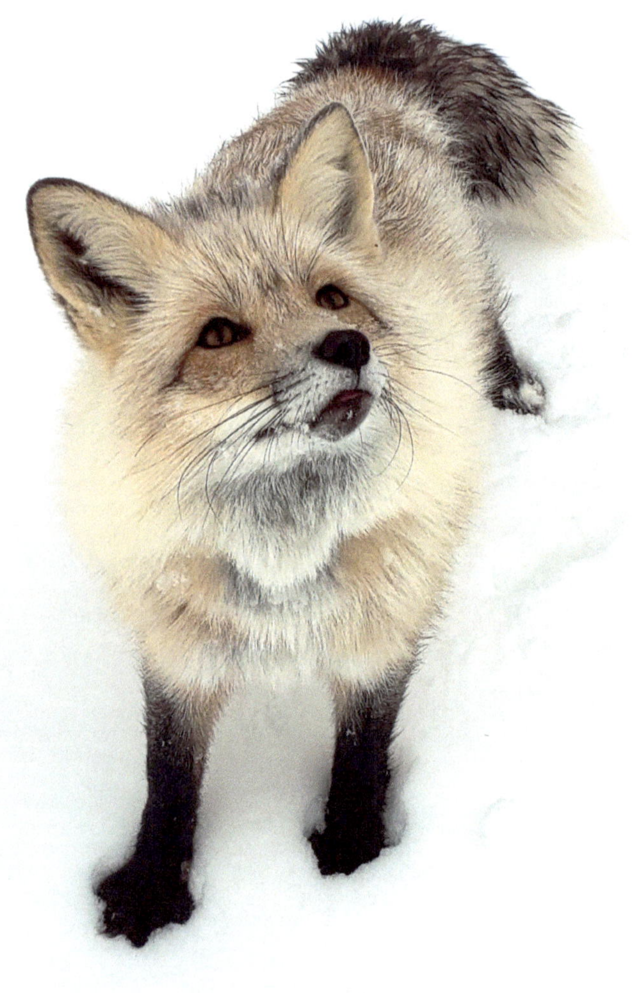

OAKLEY'S specific history is mostly unknown, but Save a Fox does know that he went in-and-out of three different homes before he was just five months old. It took a very long time for him to trust humans.

Oakley had a bit of a rough beginning and lost his trust in people. We are hoping to gain that trust back, but it will take time and consistency. Oakley is a star example of someone getting a fox from a breeder before they knew what they were getting into. Please do your research before adopting a fox—not all foxes are cut out for 'the pet life.' Before getting a fox, ask yourself: are you prepared to love and care for this fox, no matter how he turns out? The answer should be YES, or a fox isn't right for you.

MIKAYLA RAINES
Owner of Save a Fox

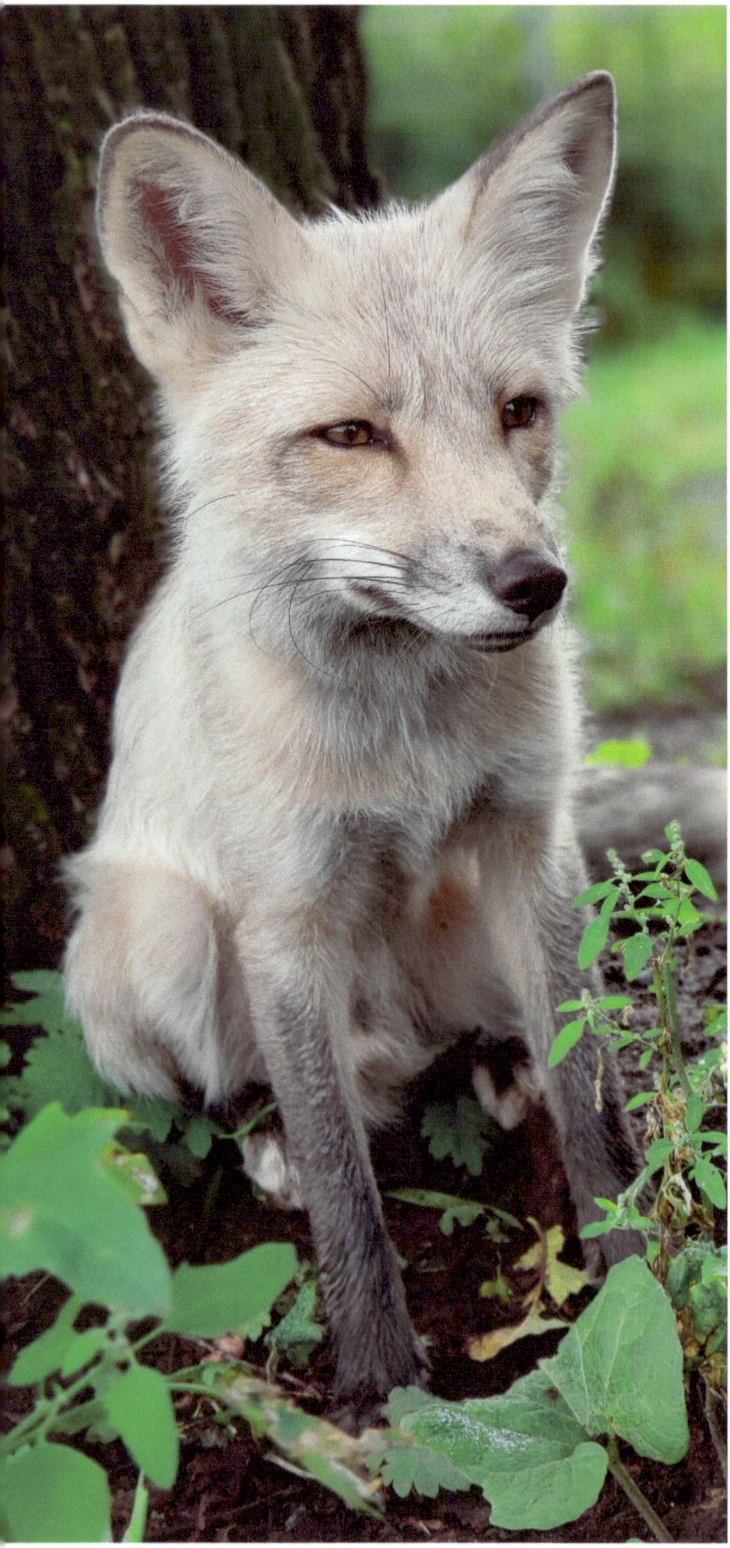

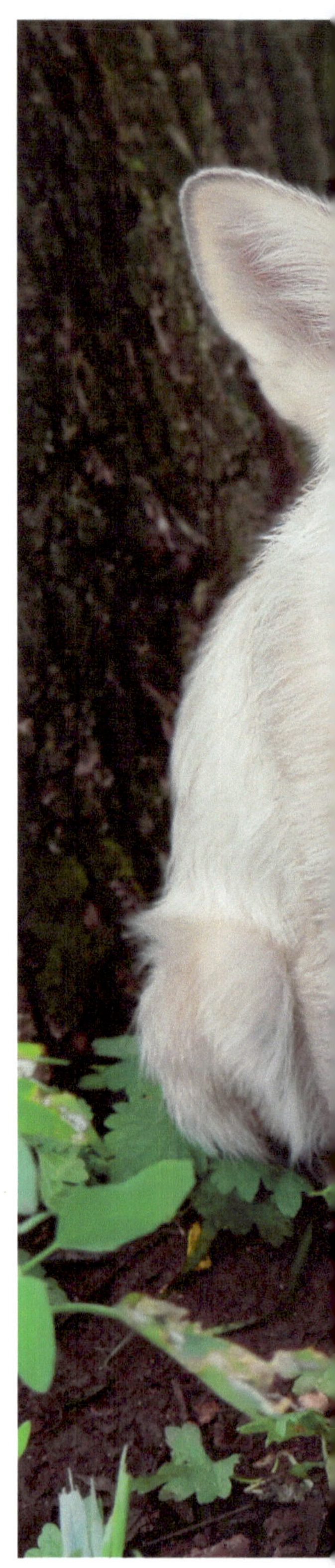

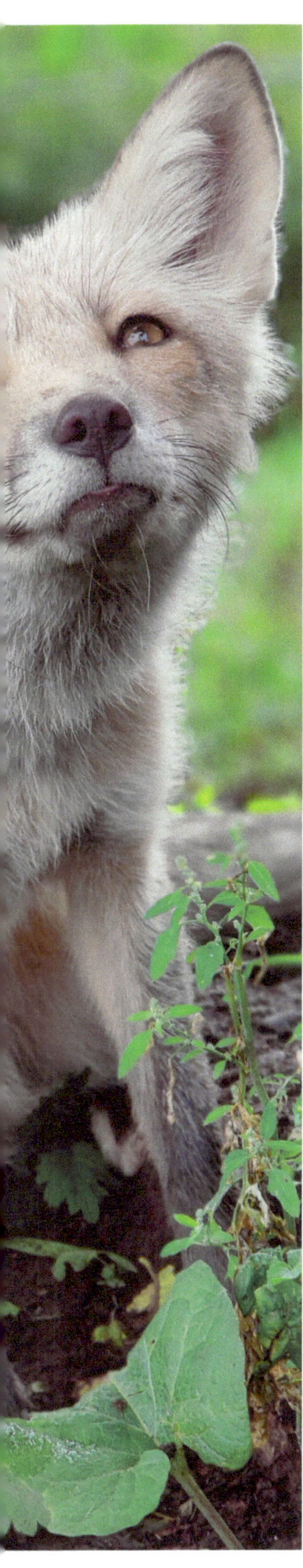

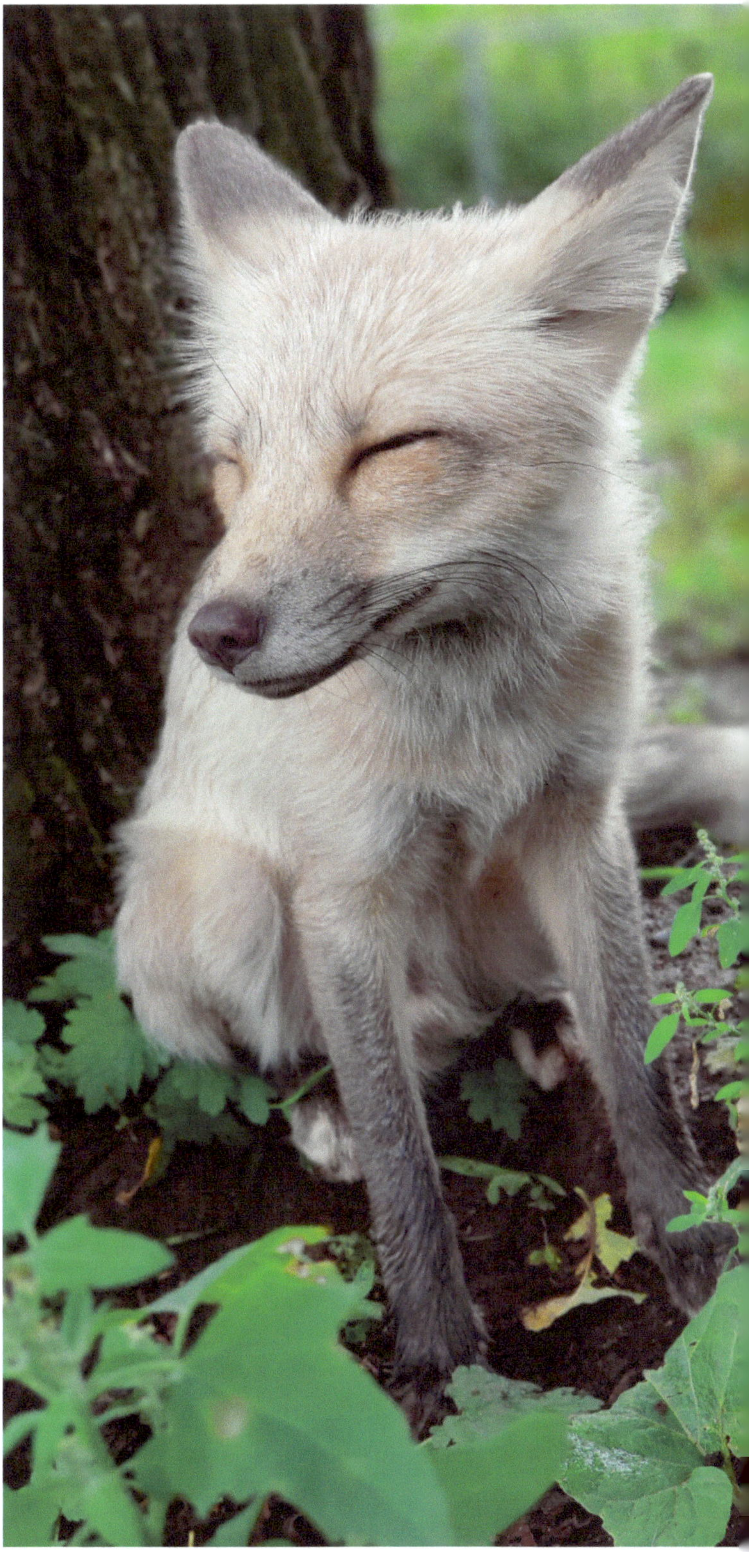

Rowyn

THE CHAMPAGNE FOX

Rowyn has always been a 'hands off' fox, as I like to call him. He's friendly, but will definitely bite for seemingly no reason—his reason is that he just likes his space. Nose boops are generally the regular physical contact between me and Rowyn, but today he wasn't up for that! Even just a nose boop made him threaten to bite me. When working with animals, one must always respect their boundaries. While a bite from a fox typically won't cause major damage, it can definitely ruin your day!

REANNA COLE
Rowyn's owner and Website and Social Media Assistant at Save a Fox

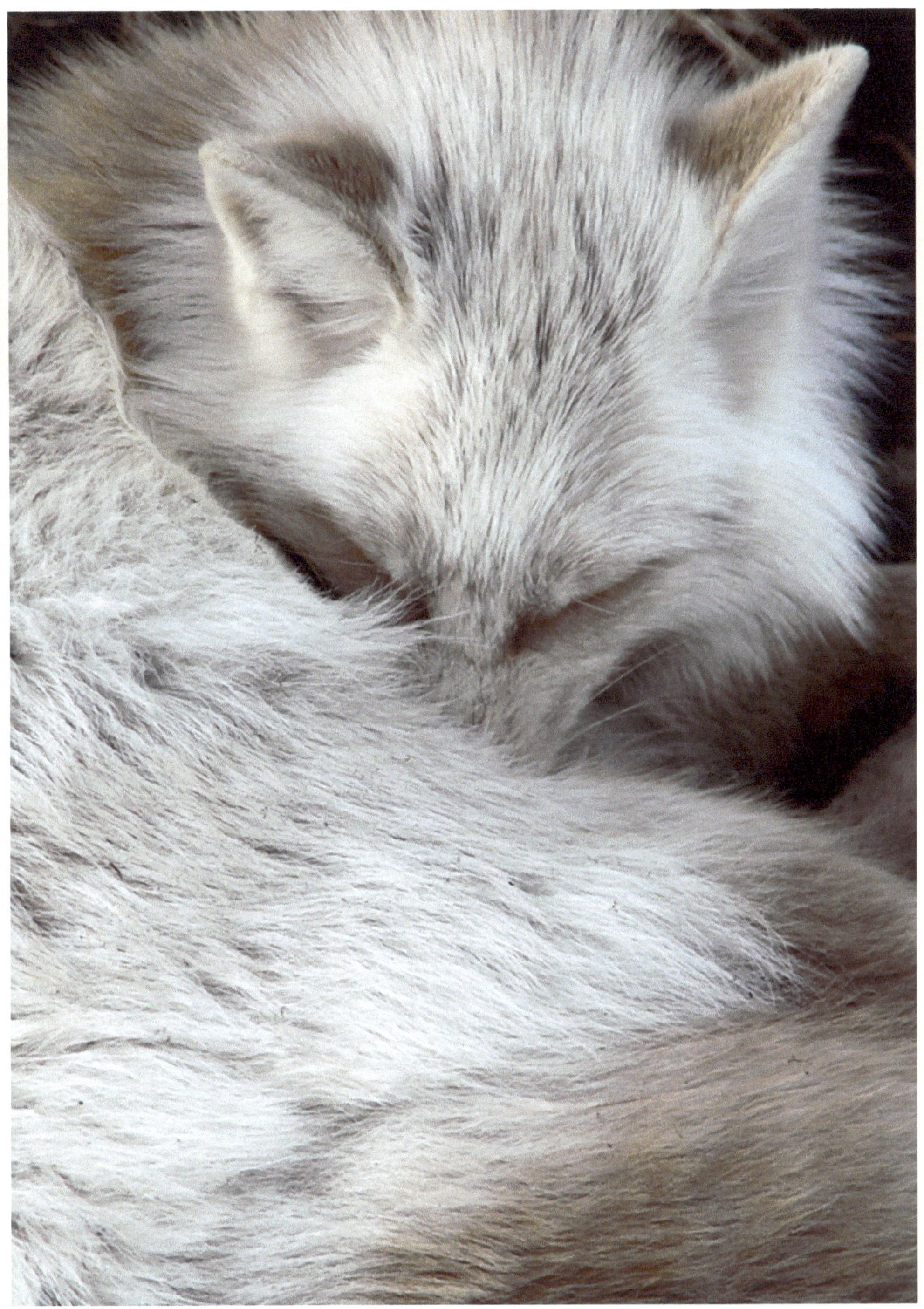

R O W Y N was rescued from a fur farm as a kit, and adopted from Save a Fox in July 2017. He now lives in Oklahoma with his new owner, Reanna, and a female fox named Thystle, who was also adopted from Save a Fox. Rowyn might be the son of Bongo *(page 22)*, a breeder fox who was rescued from the same fur farm several years after Rowyn.

THE CHAMPAGNE FOX, sometimes called the "pink fox" or "pink champagne fox," is a color mutation of the red fox that is characterized by light blonde or peach-hued fur, a pink nose, and ice blue eyes. The champagne fox color is only found in captivity, and it is popular in the pet trade.

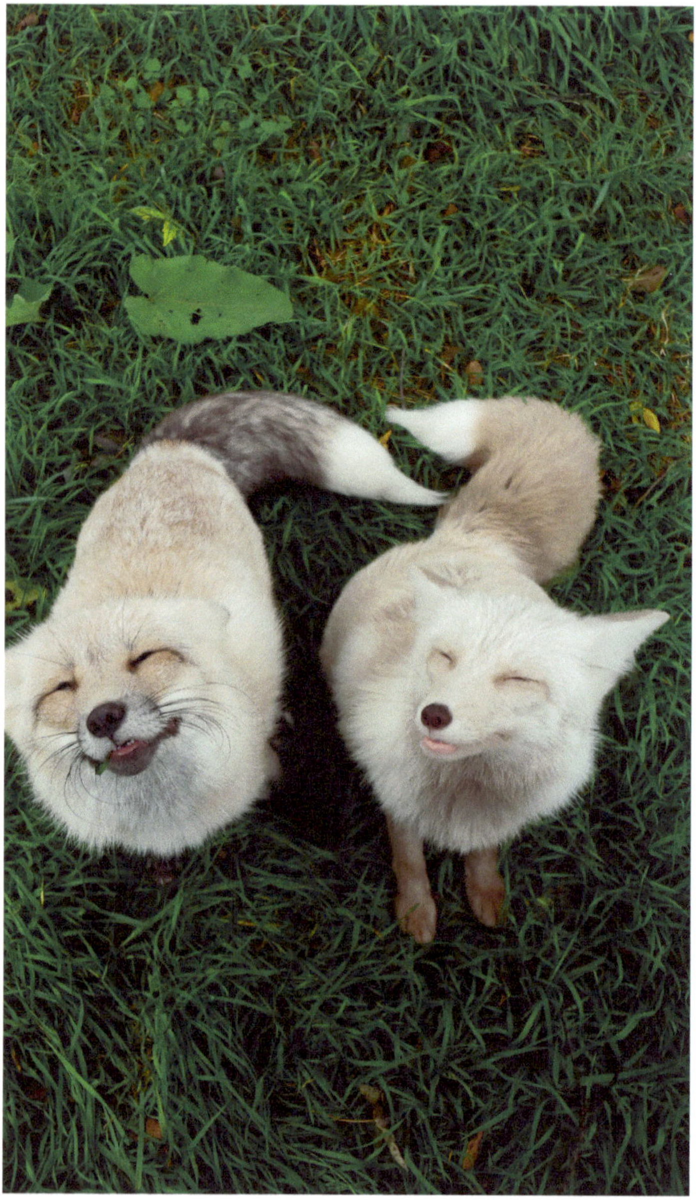

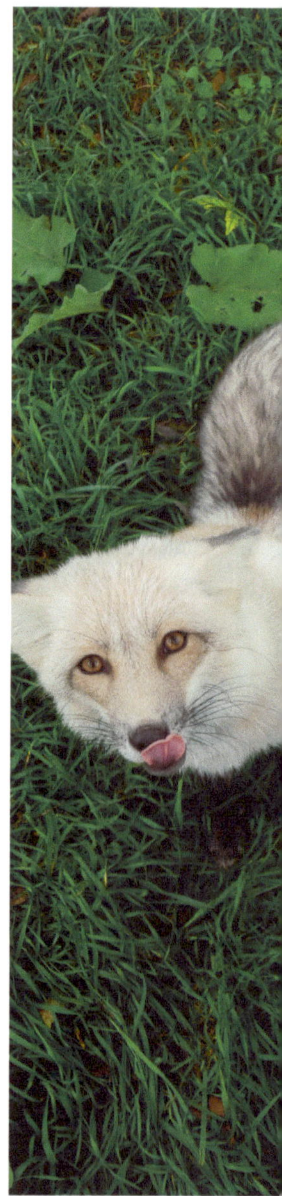

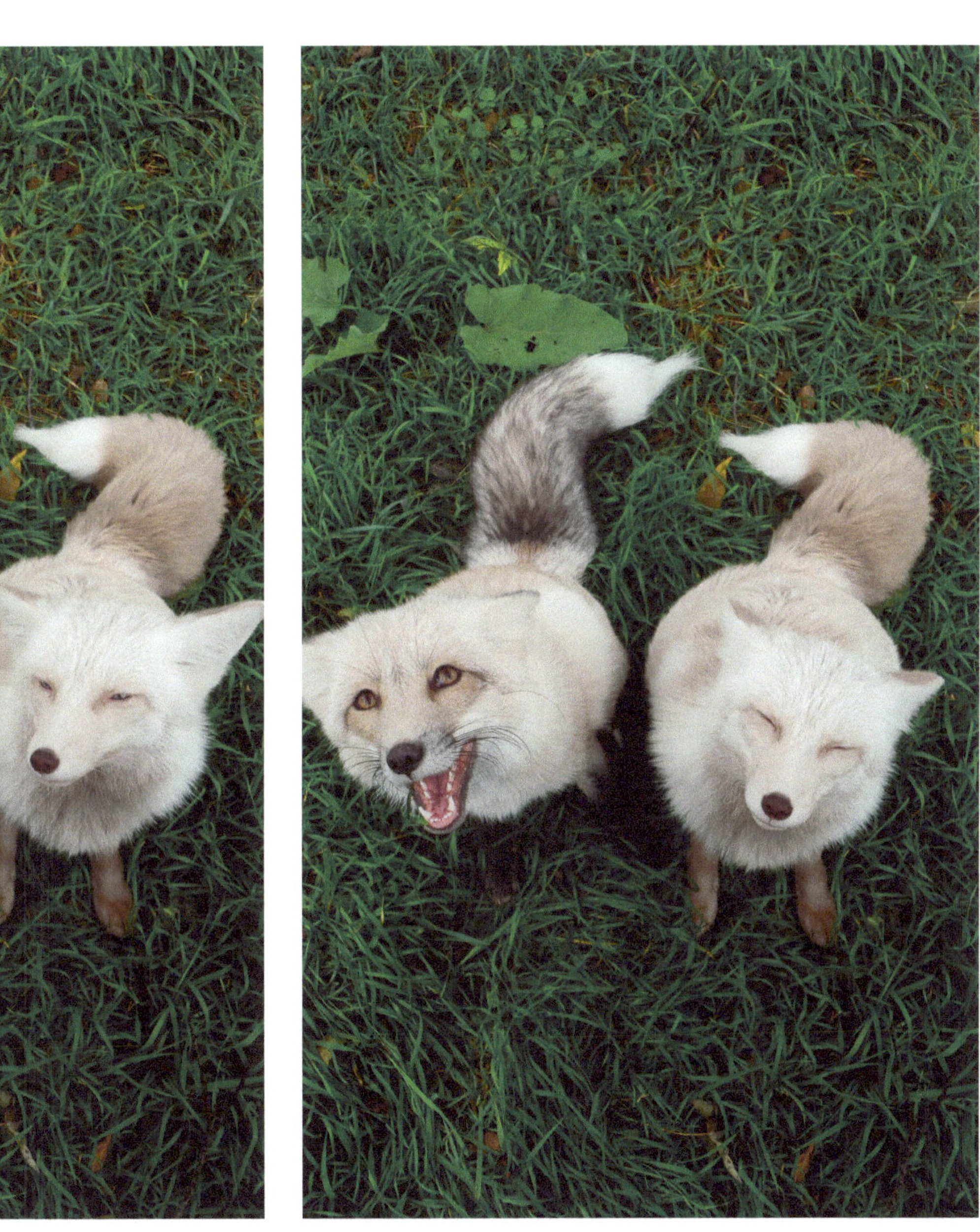

R O W Y N *(right)* and Oakley *(left)* pose for the camera, waiting for treats. "It's tough to get Rowyn to show off those baby blue eyes because they're more sensitive to the sun," Mikayla Raines said. *Read Oakley's story on page 80.*

Tonia was a part of Save a Fox's very first fur farm rescue litter, born in the spring of 2016. Tonia's mother, Envy, rejected her and the rest of her littermates when they were 10 days old. Mother foxes living in fur farms often stop caring for their kits shortly after giving birth, most likely because they don't feel like the environment is safe for raising a litter. Luckily for Tonia and her brothers, Clyde and Notchi, Save a Fox contacted the farmer and managed to rescue the litter from the fur farm, where they would not have survived into adulthood without their mother's care. When the Save a Fox team discovered that Envy was scheduled to be pelted (skinned for her pelt) that winter since she rejected her litter, they stepped in again, rescuing her as well. Envy was adopted by Faux Fur and Friends, a Florida-based fox rescue.

Today, Tonia lives a full and happy life at the sanctuary, where she rules as queen of her fox yard.

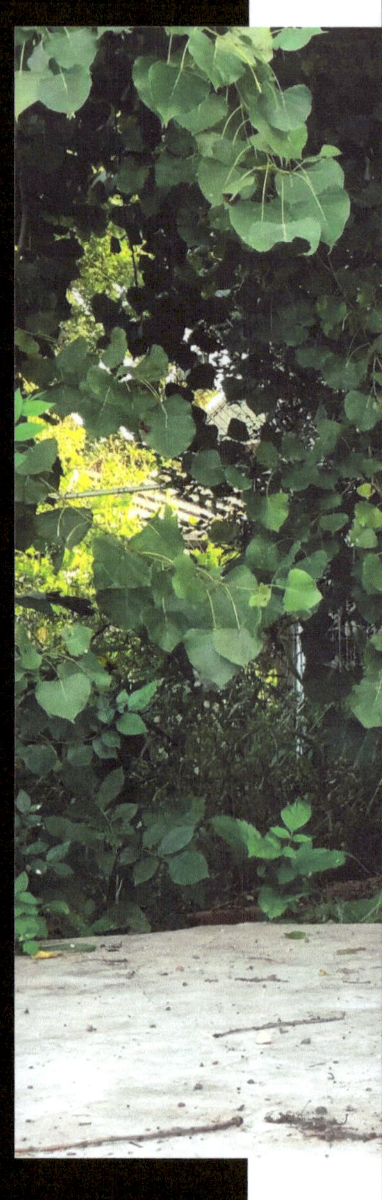

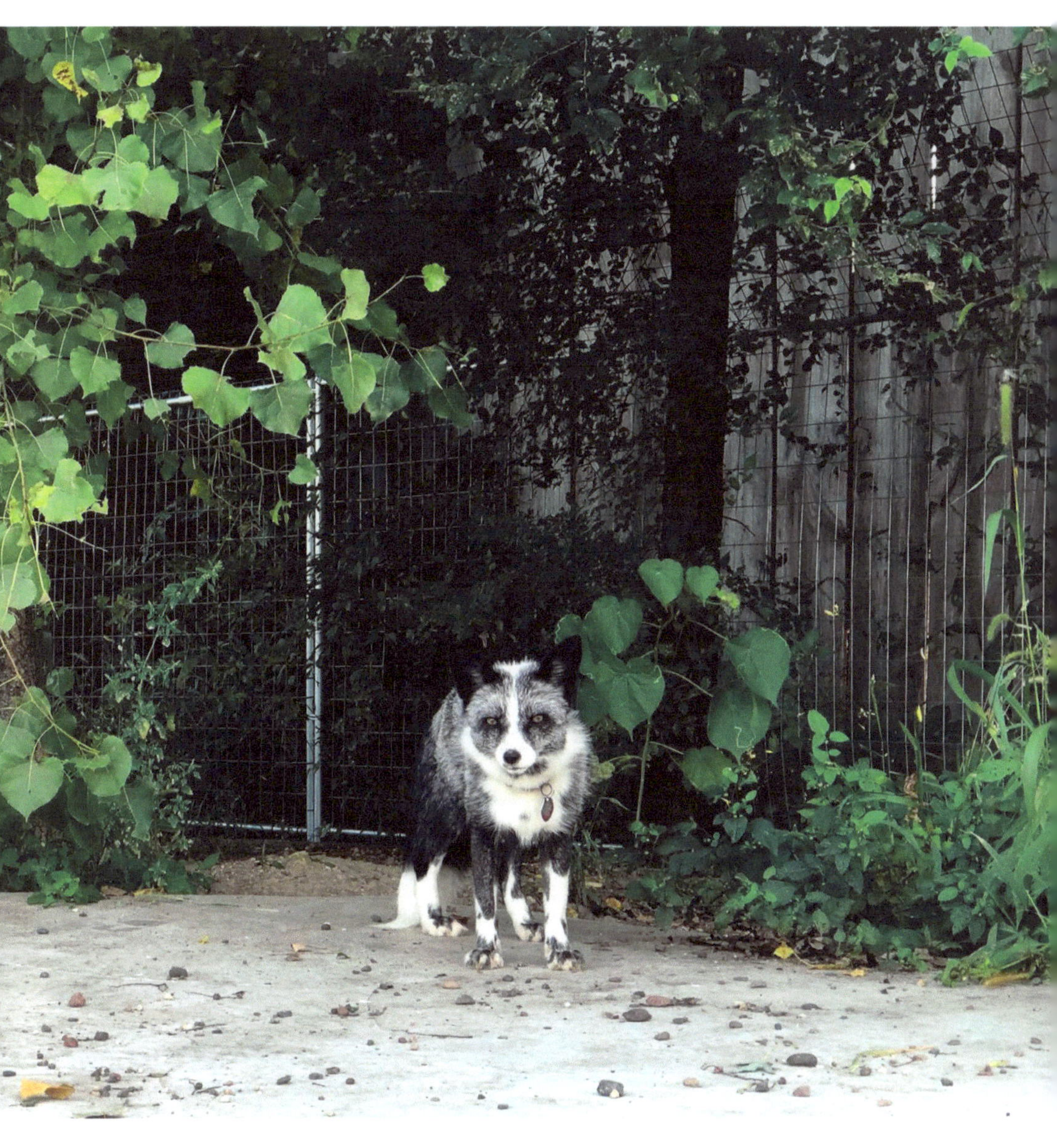

TONIA
THE SILVER WHITE MARK FOX

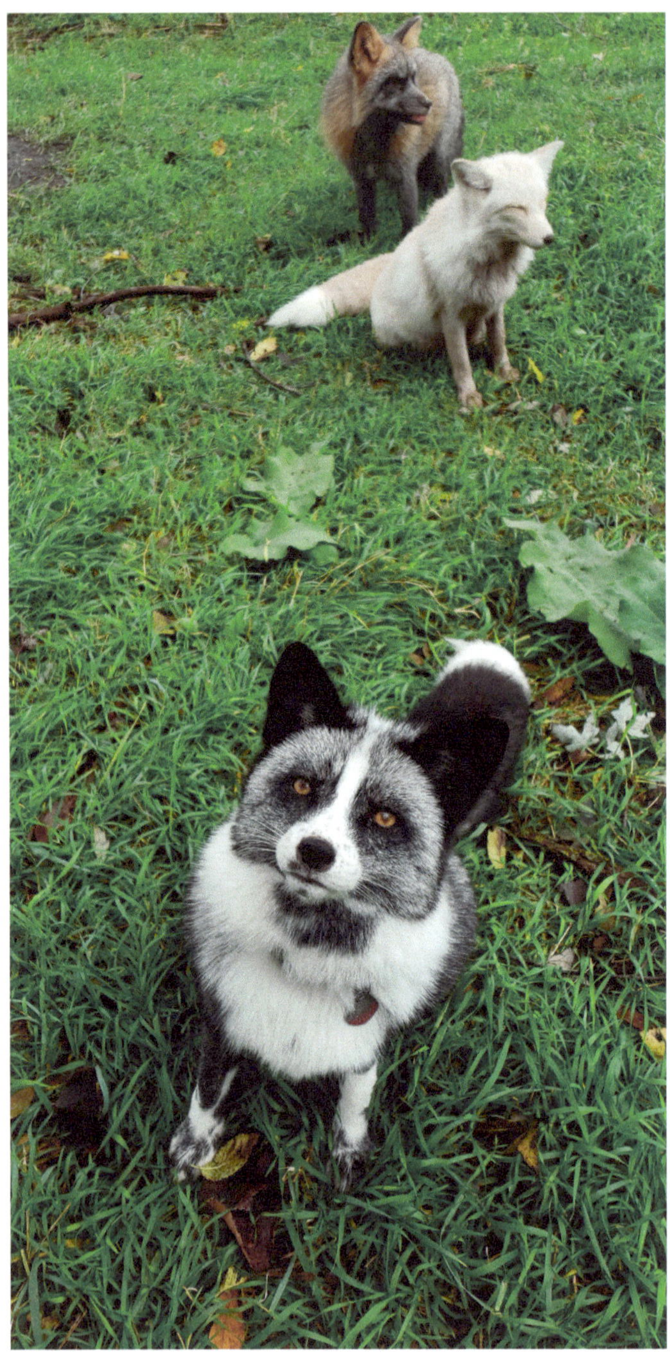

T O N I A has earned the nickname "Ice T" because, as Mikayla puts it, "as cute is she is, she is cold as ice if you aren't her groupie!" She often is housed with Valentine and Rowyn *(above)*. Only one female is allowed in a fox yard at a time because female foxes are more likely to fight with each other. *See Valentine's story on page 96, and Rowyn's story on page 86.*

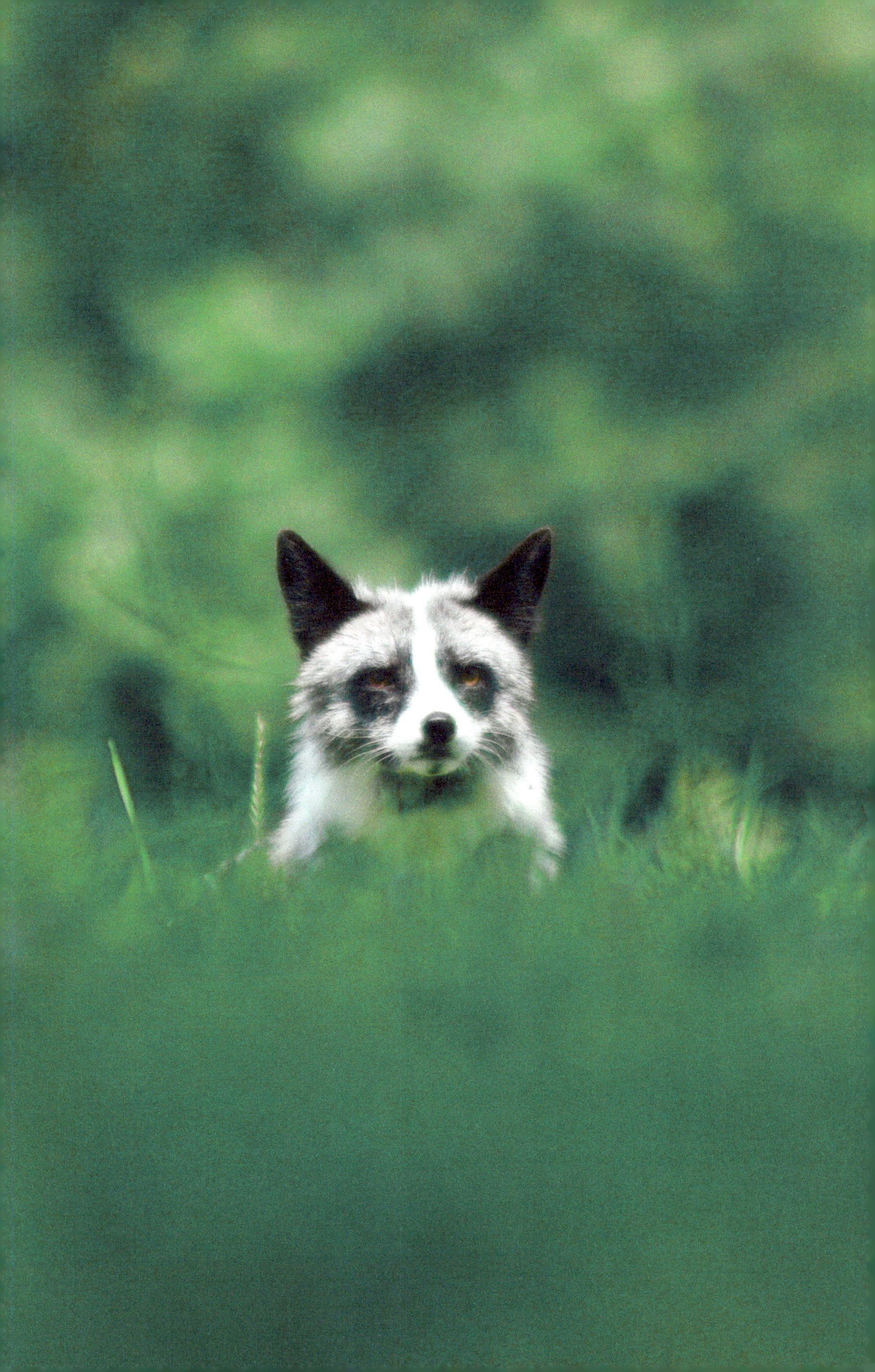

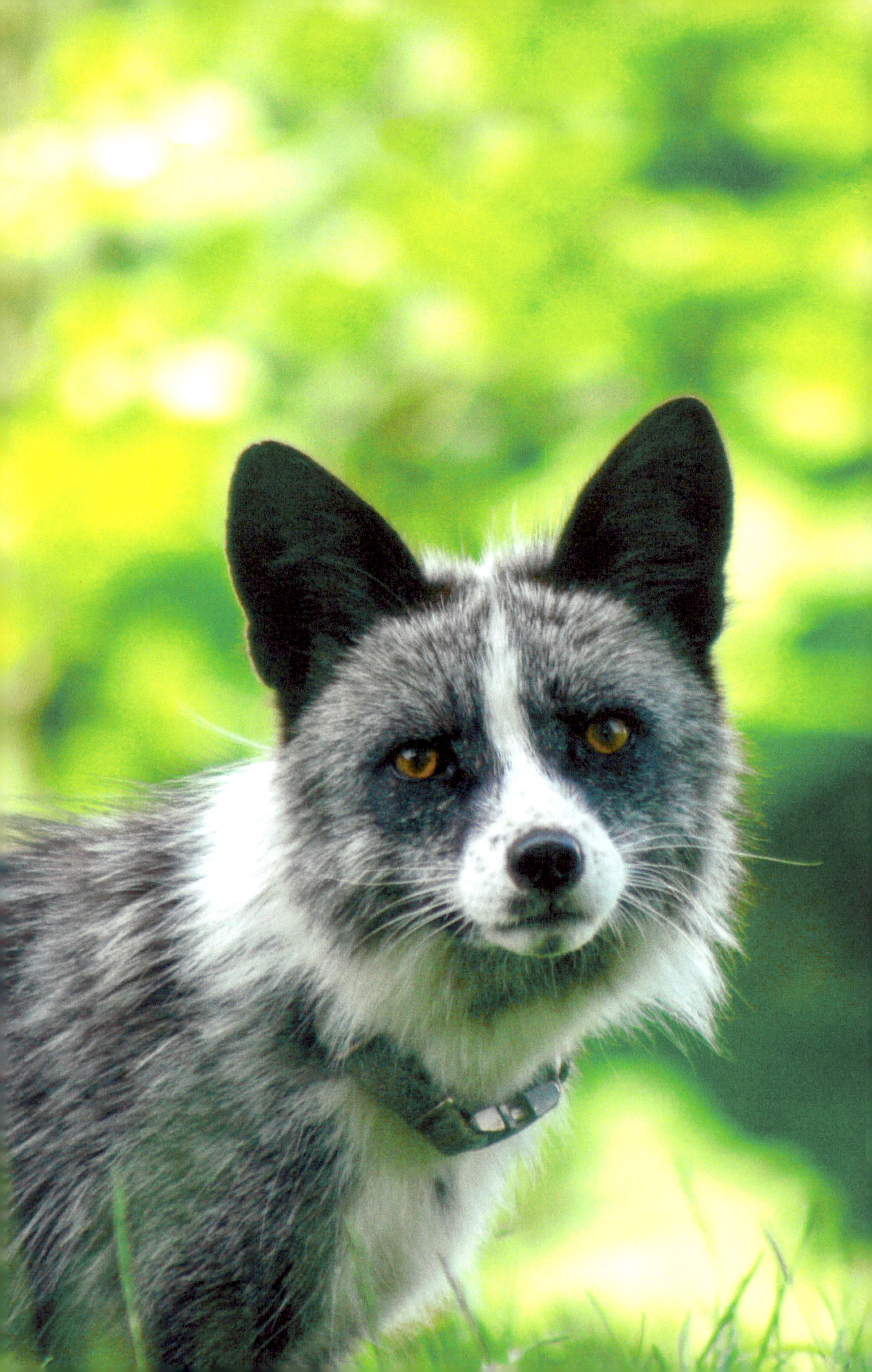

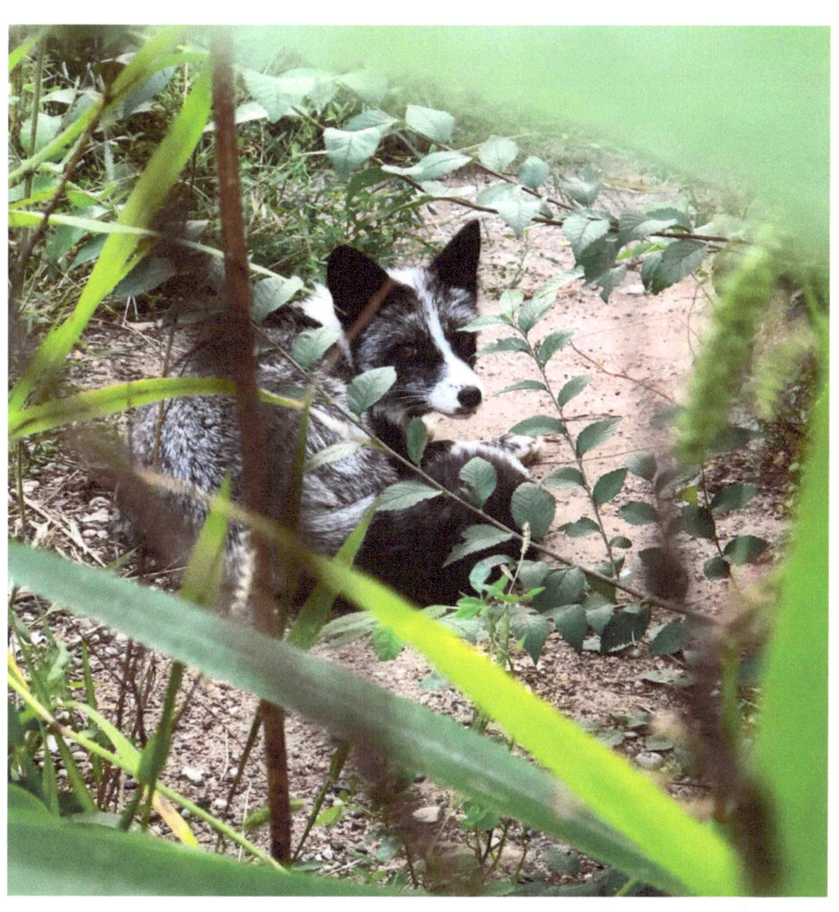

> ## 66
>
> *(Above)* This is how taking photos of Tonia usually goes for me. She's only a fan of Mikayla being in her space bubble, unless you bring treats!
>
> **ALEXIS HOWARD**
> *Live-in animal caretaker at Save a Fox*
>
> ## 99

> **"** Val is walking and being given a house and toys for the first time ever [...] How an animal that has been through so much could have so much trust is astonishing. **"**

MIKAYLA RAINES
Owner of Save a Fox

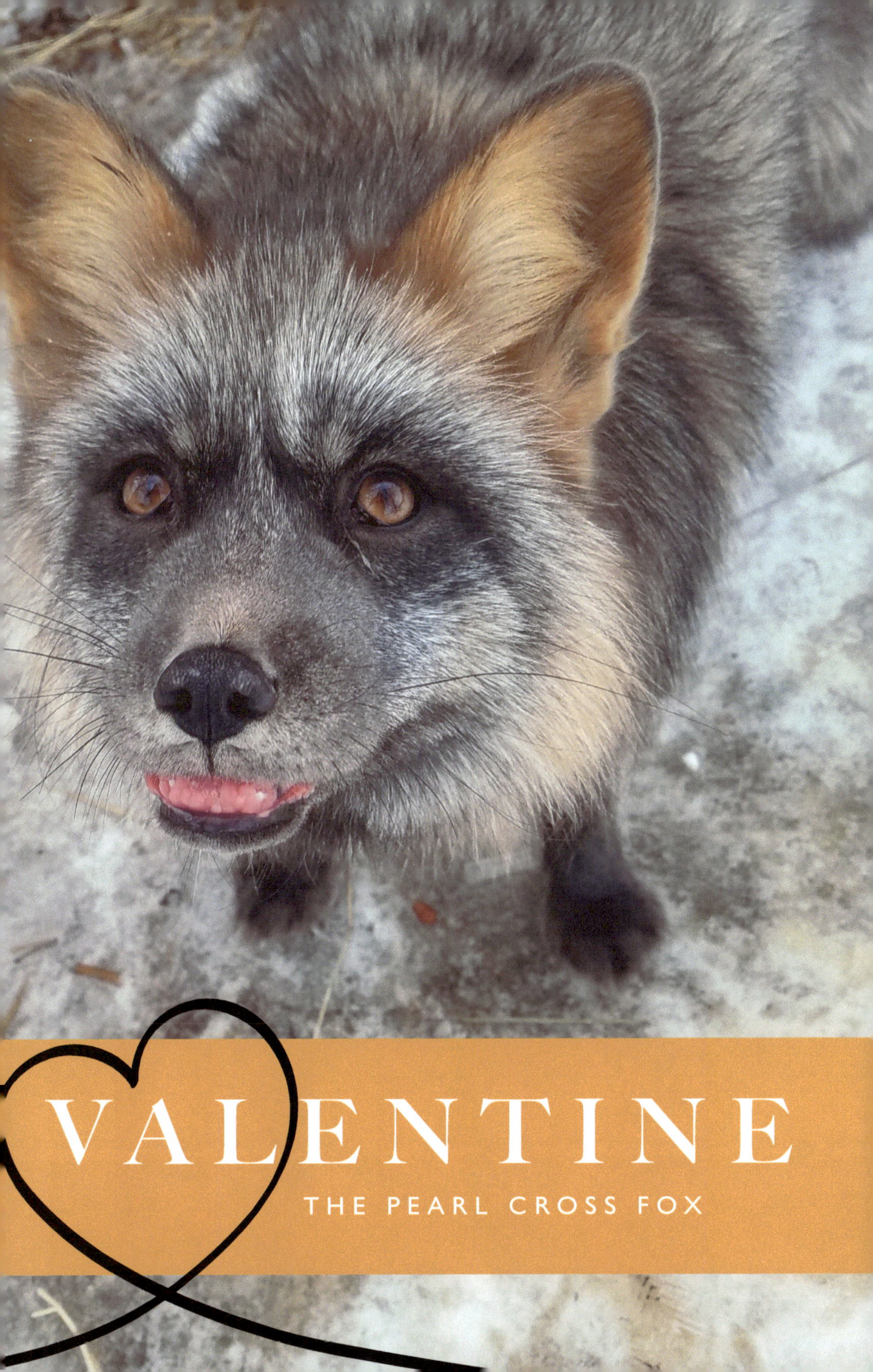
VALENTINE
THE PEARL CROSS FOX

Vixie

THE SILVER FOX

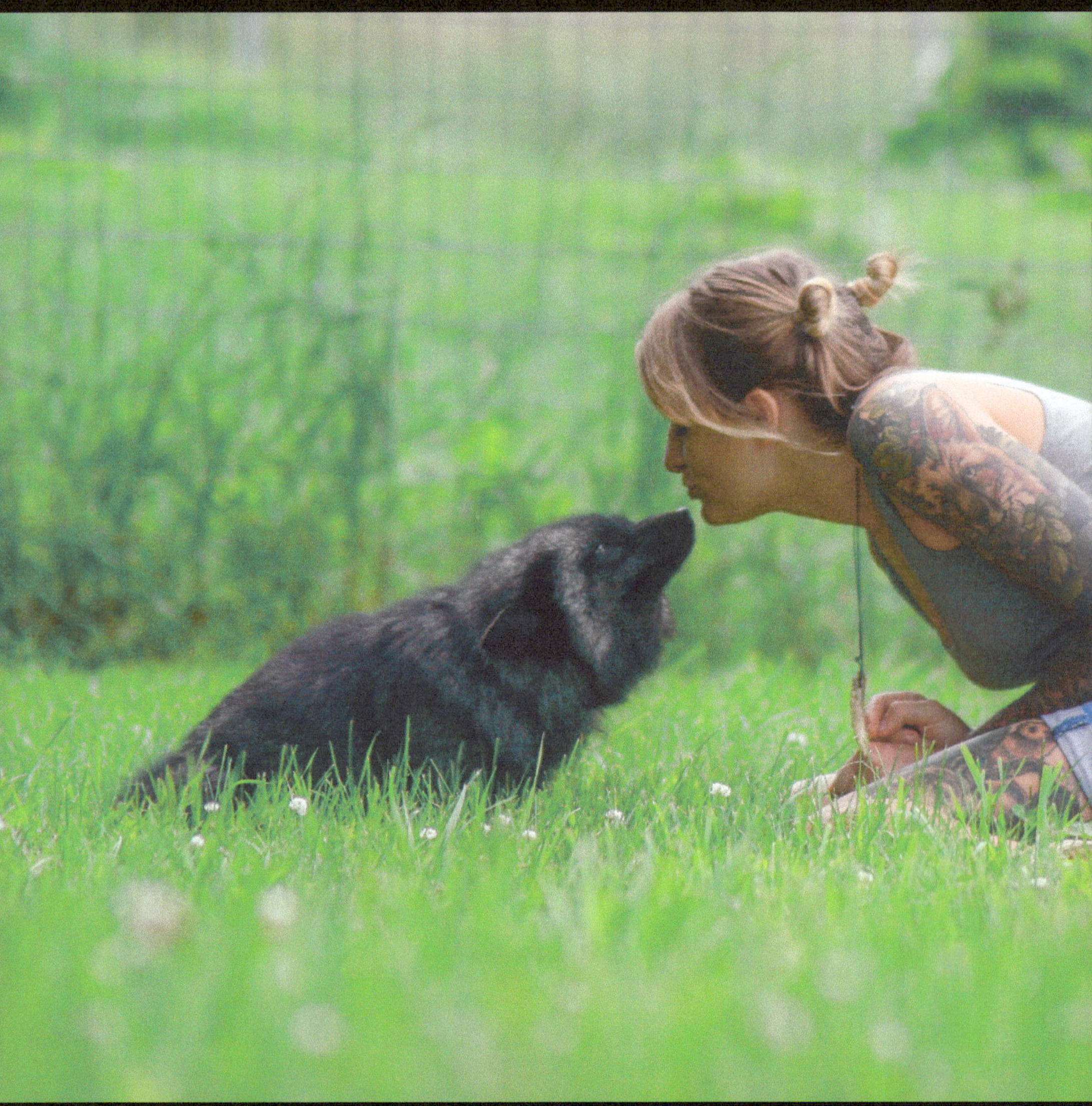

VIXIE came to the rescue as an emergency surrender after her owner was arrested. It's believed that she spent the beginning of her life indoors in very poor living conditions. Now, she is best friends with Muttias, another silver fox who was surrendered around the same time as her and helped her come out of her shell. *Read more about Muttias on page 76.*

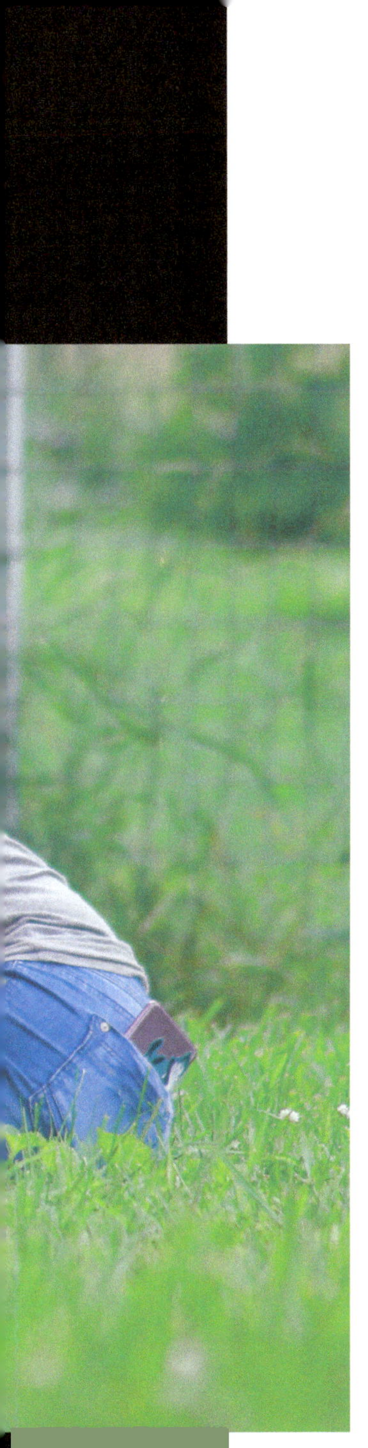

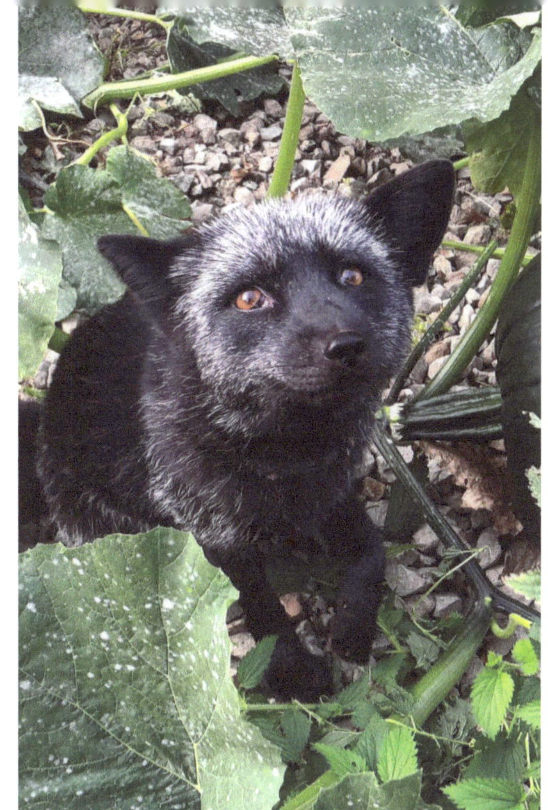

> **"**
>
> Our newest surrender, Vixie. She is finally starting to come out of her shell, and show some excitement for attention. It took about a week to get a tail-wag out of her.

MIKAYLA RAINES
Owner of Save a Fox

(Written one week after Vixie was surrendered)

> **"**

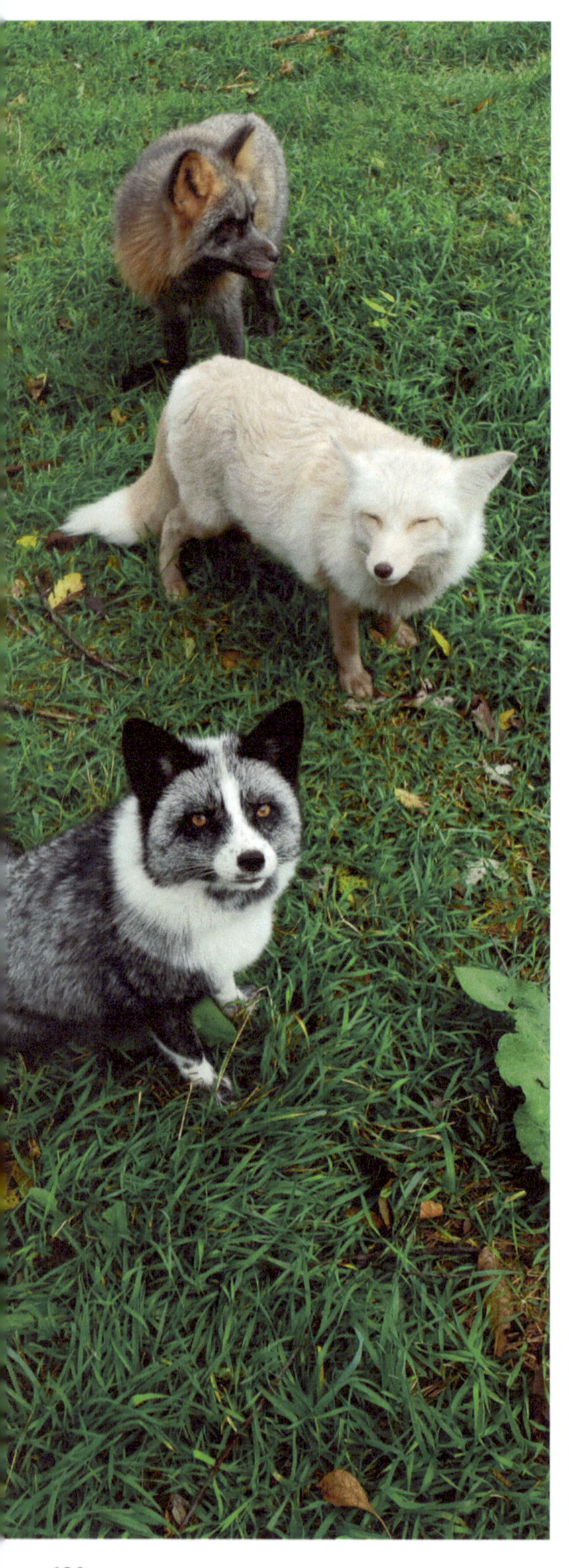

FOX SPECIES AND COLORS

FRONT TO BACK: Tonia the silver white mark fox *(page 90)*, Rowyn the champagne fox *(page 86)*, and Valentine the pearl cross fox *(page 96)*.

RIGHT PAGE: Oakley, the fire and ice fox *(page 80)*.

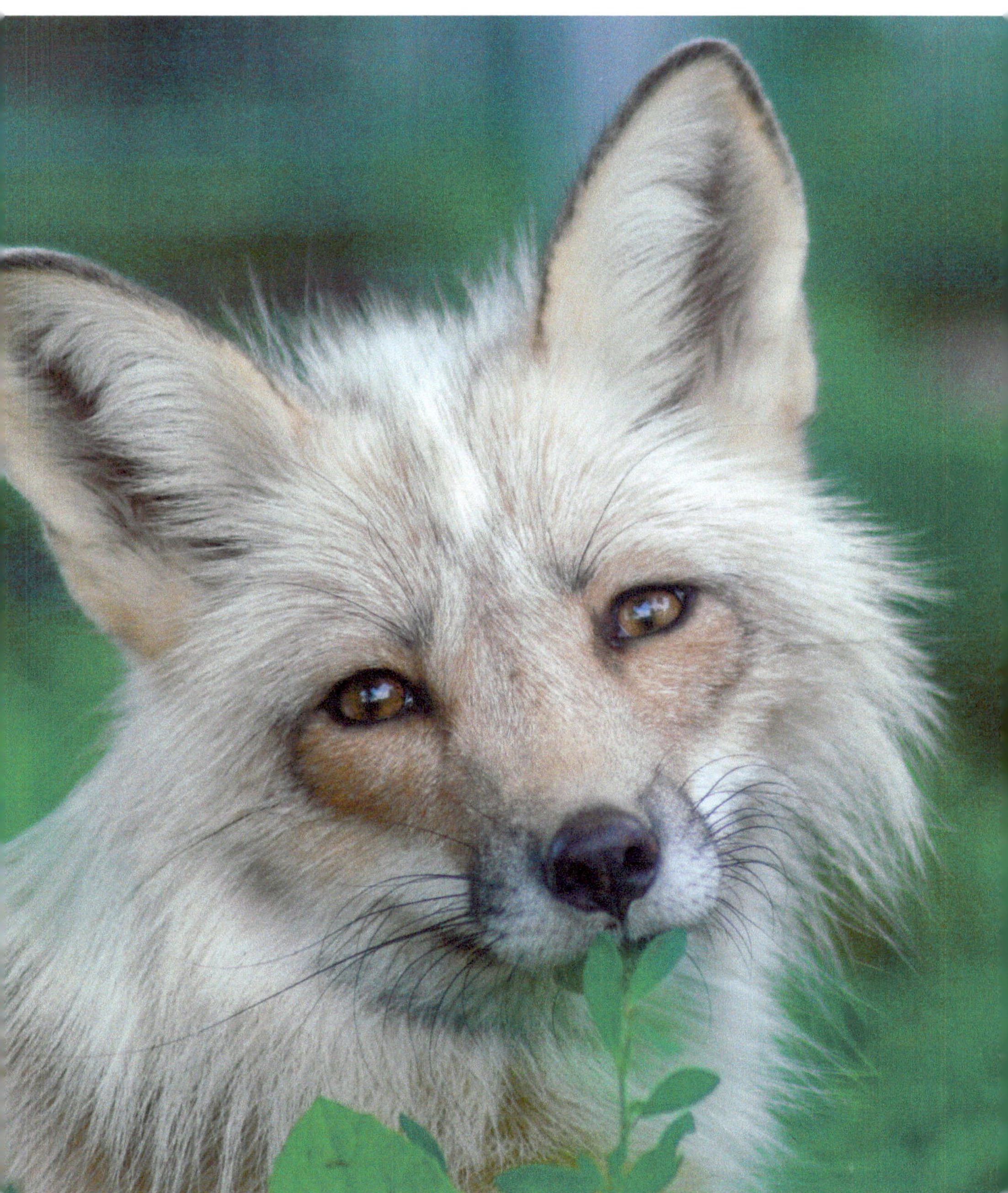

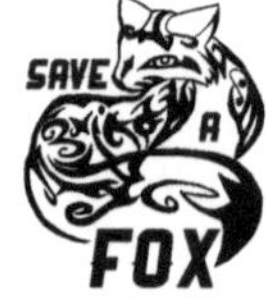